The First Book OF Microcomputers

THE HOME COMPUTER OWNER'S BEST FRIEND

Robert Moody

HAYDEN BOOK COMPANY, INC.
Rochelle Park, New Jersey

Without the strong support of a few good friends, this book would not have come about. I am dedicating this book to them: to Sue Olsen, my typist, who has the fastest fingers in the west; Phil Roark, who created my character, Willy, and did the cartoons; Robin Weckesser, who had such a steady hand with the illustrations; Lynne Lee, my typesetter who never sleeps; Dr. Jerry Fox for his support on the technical side; Mike Trioca on software; and, last but not least, to my wife, Karolynn, and two children, Justin and Shannon, who put up with me over the course of writing it. I love you all and thank you.

ISBN 0-8104-5121-2
Library of Congress Catalog Card Number 78-63396

| 4 | 5 | 6 | 7 | 8 | 9 | PRINTING |

| 79 | 80 | 81 | 82 | 83 | 84 | 85 | 86 | YEAR |

CONTENTS

I.

INTRODUCTION —
YOUR COMPUTER IS WAITING

Computers are now personal! Whoever you are, whatever you do — whether housewife, small businessman, student, professional, musician, or real estate salesperson — computers are being made and sold at prices *you* can afford for applications beneficial to *you*. A personal computer will open possibilities that will almost certainly change your lifestyle at work and play.

You may ask yourself, "What is a personal computer? The only computers I've ever seen have been huge. How can anyone afford to put such an expensive piece of equipment in their home, and where would I put it?" Like Willy over there, almost everyone's first impression of a computer is of a monstrous machine, owned only by wealthy businesses, that towers over them, overseeing all and doing all. This may have been an accurate impression 10 to 15 years ago, but not today. The technology that has been developed over the past few years has not only reduced the physical size of computers, but has lowered computer prices tremendously.

You have been in direct contact with computers in one way or another most

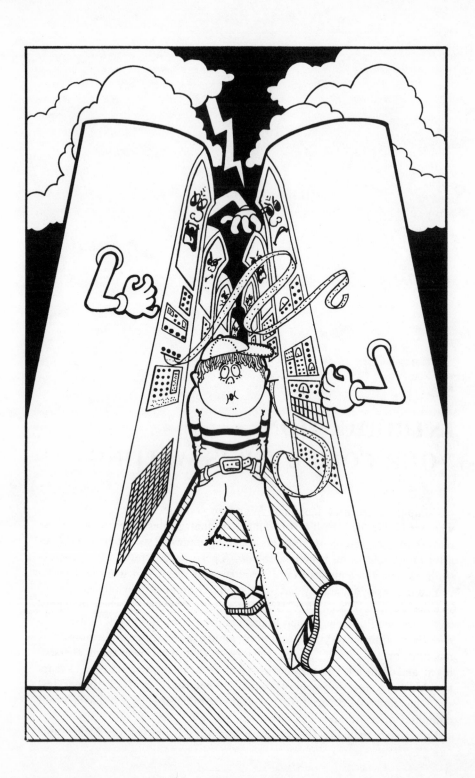

of your life without knowing it. For example, many school records and schedules are stored in computers. Your family or business tax returns are processed by a computer. Most major department stores handle their buying, stocking, and billing by computer. Many newspapers and magazines are set in type under computer control. All credit card purchases are handled by computer. Every check written is processed by computer. Dentist, doctor, hospital, gas, and phone bills are handled by computer. The reasons why are obvious.

In a city the size of San Francisco, for instance, it would take a tremendous amount of manpower to process all the checks San Francisco banks receive in one day, or to log the number and duration of all phone calls made in one day. Computing power is needed to handle that amount of information, and that kind of computing power is at your fingertips today.

This book was written principally for two reasons: (1) to bring a little light into misunderstandings about computers and (2) to show its readers how personal computers can help them in their everyday lives.

A BRIEF, BRIEF HISTORY

The first digital computer, ENIAC, was built at the University of Pennsylvania in 1946. It filled a large room (1,500 square feet), and weighed 30 tons. ENIAC used vacuum tubes (18,500) to store ten-digit numbers. The tubes were so short-lived, ENIAC would not run for more than seven or eight minutes without a tube failure. Special vacuum tubes were developed to cut down its tremendous power requirements (130,000 watts), so the machine could run at a cooler temperature. After constant and deliberate work, ENIAC would run for several days without a tube failure.

Constant improvement over the years made ENIAC a very useful machine. The U.S. census of 1950 was possible largely because of ENIAC, which was retired in 1955.

It took a tremendous amount of knowledge to operate and talk to ENIAC and its early relatives — ENVAC, IAS, UNIVAC, and the early IBM machines. Engineers and scientists labored for months to understand and implement their usefulness.

The ENIAC computer cost more than half a million dollars (that's 1950 dollars!) to develop. Today you can buy the same computing power for under $1000 (that's 1978 dollars).

Through constant improvement these early computers grew into the most influential tool of the twentieth century. The advancement of many important fields could not have come about without them. Medicine, communications, space exploration, travel, and mass merchandizing (to mention just a few) could not have come as far as they have without computer technology.

3

COMPUTERS TODAY — CHIPS OFF THE OLD BLOCK

The average person today, young or old, can use and enjoy with ease what computer technology has developed for him. What cost a half a million dollars and months of implementation and study in 1950 can be purchased at a fraction of the cost and be used and understood in a matter of a few hours. This is possible solely through the development of integrated circuits, in which circuit components are reduced in size and packed closely in small areas.

The *computer on a chip* was developed in the early 1970's by Intel Corp. of Santa Clara, California. The 8080, as they named it, took the place of many integrated circuits. To give you a little comparison, this small electronic device would have replaced all 18,800 vacuum tubes in the ENIAC computer of 1950. Many cousins of the 8080 are in use in microcomputers today. You will hear of them often: the 6800, the Z80, the 6502, and others.

Computer languages have been developed over the years to make it possible for anyone to use these powerful, compact machines. What took months of study and understanding to be able to accomplish with the earlier computers can now be done with simple English terms today.

INTRODUCTION TO A FRIEND

I would like you to meet a friend of mine, Willy. He is going to help me tell you about microcomputers. He was inspired by an acquaintance I had when my computer store first opened. This person would hang around all day asking questions, trying to understand what these things, personal computers, were all about. He is the main reason I have written this book. He is one of the thousands of kids who have the inquisitive mind to reach out to a new subject and then drag their parents and friends along with their useful, probing questions.

I have written this, as well, for you parents who might pick this book up. It should keep your interest as well, and help you stay one step in front of your kids.

ABOUT THIS BOOK

In this book the segments of computing are broken down into easily understood blocks. First, I will start off with a glossary of useful terms in programming and software. We will discuss what it takes to communicate with a home computer, some of the rules, so to speak, to follow, and the language that the computer talks in.

Next I will give you another glossary of useful terms on hardware, the

5

equipment itself. I will talk about what makes up a home computer and basically how it works. Another section will be an interview between Willy and his computer. The computer will let Willy explore the inner workings of what a home computer does and how computers interact with each other.

I will finish the book with answers to the most-often asked questions that I receive, "What do you do with a home computer?", and a chapter on what's next in personal computing. I will give a review of the more popular periodicals treating home computing, as well as a list of computer stores and computer clubs.

This book is your beginning in personal computing. Your first friend in computing. There are many other friends waiting for you — on the book racks in your local store, in the computer clubs near you, and, especially, behind the counter of any computer store you enter.

II.

THE BEST SOFTWARE
BUZZWORDS

The first major hurdle you have to face in home computing is learning the lingo. As a group, computer people have probably abused the English language more than those in any other industry. Our specialized language has overgrown, trying to distinguish word by word, to the point where English-speaking people have great difficulty deciphering our apparent "gibberish." If it were up to me I would like to start all over again and use terms that everyone would be able to understand and not have to adapt to a complete new way of conversing. I can't do that, so all you folks who are reading this book to gain an insight as to what personal computers are all about will have to forget the accepted definitions of some of the words that you have learned in school and take up *Computerese.* It's not going to be that difficult to do — just deprogram your brain and THINK COMPUTER.

The first computer terms we will deal with describe the way we talk to our computers. *Software,* as it is called, is the list of instructions we give to the computer to do a job. It is also the way the computer takes this list and converts it to the language it knows.

BIT: The smallest unit of measure in a computer word; several bits make up a byte, or a computer word.

BYTE: The space which a letter or digit (one character) takes up in a computer. Space in a computer is measured in bytes. A <u>megabyte</u> is a million bytes.

ASCII: <u>A</u>merican <u>S</u>tandard <u>C</u>ode for <u>I</u>nformation <u>I</u>nterchange: this is a seven-bit code that defines letters and numbers that the computer uses as its input.

ALPHANUMERIC:
Information that is made up of letters (the alphabet) and digits (numbers).

INPUT:
The information that goes **IN** to your computer system. The computer's "food."

PROGRAM:
A list of instructions to the computer, telling it what to do and when to do it.

DATA = The information that gets **WORKED OVER** when your program runs. Data is all the information you have your computer use, everything that you put into your computer to store and retrieve.

OUTPUT = Using the program you have put into your computer as the instructions and the data for information, the output is the finished product your computer system produces.

BASIC = Beginers All-Purpose Symbolic Instructional Code = A "language" that you will use to write your programs for your computer, using English words and phrases.

FORTRAN = Formula Translation = another computer language used in programming that is composed of English words and symbols for instructions.

III.

PROGRAMMING

The best way to start this chapter off is by defining the term *program*. A program is a list of instructions that we give a computer so it can do a specific job for us. Though there are certain rules that we have to follow, it's no more difficult to write or follow a computer program than it is to bake a cake from scratch ingredients. Both take time and practice to be done correctly, but they can be done.

The computer is a machine that has been designed to know two things, on or off. However simple this may sound, it is true. Knowing that a combination of circuits is either on or off, enables the computer to "recognize" letters and numbers.

Programs contain strange and familiar words (and familiar numbers). Let's break down what we in the computer industry call a *word*. First of all, the name is changed. It's not a word but a *byte,* and it's not a complete word like those you are reading, but a single character or number. Confusing!? It will get better.

byte: A SINGLE CHARACTER OR NUMBER

bit: ONE PORTION OF THE WHOLE BYTE

AS WE KNOW IT
THE CAPITAL LETTER

AS THE COMPUTER
SEES IT

A = **I000000I** ← a byte

bit = JUST ONE
OF THE SEVEN ZERO'S
OR ONE'S

FROM ASCII TO BASIC

If you examine the first illustration, I think we can clear up your uncertainty. The normal alphabet as we know it has to be broken down to a simple code so a computer can understand it. This code is called the ASCII character set. ASCII stands for **AMERICAN STANDARD CODE for INFORMATION INTERCHANGE.** This code plays a very important part in the role of conversing with a computer. Because it is a standard, we can safely say that all digital computers use the ASCII code to communicate with humans.

The ASCII code is made up of seven bits. These one's and zero's, when in certain combinations of seven, will make up our English alphabet and numbers. Being computer people and tending towards being difficult at times, we have added one small detail to this code: an eighth bit. This one or zero is placed in front of the other seven and called a *parity bit.* This parity bit allows the computer to double check the information we have put in. Depending on how the computer and the sending device are set up, the sending device chooses the eighth bit so that the total number of ones in the byte is even (if it is using even parity) or odd (if it is using odd parity).

Once the computer has received the byte from the sending device, it can check to see if the parity is the same as when the byte was sent. If not, an error occurred in transmitting the byte or character from the sending device to the computer. If all this has confused you, don't be alarmed, you really don't need to know it anyway. Just think of a parity bit as a way the computer checks to see if the character received is the one we sent. That's all!

Getting back to bits and bytes! The ASCII code, which you will hear about throughout this book, is listed in the back of this book in the appendix in a table that shows the alphanumerics (alphabet and numbers 0 through 9) and the symbols that we will use in programming.

Having a special code that the computer understands isn't enough for us computer people to confuse you. What we have also done is make it necessary to learn a special language using our standard alphabet to talk to computers. No! It's not Southern Mongolian, but something a little easier than English.

The language that most home computers use is called BASIC. BEGIN-NERS ALL-PURPOSE SYMBOLIC INSTRUCTIONAL CODE is what BASIC stands for. This home computer language is designed as an interpreter. It is interpretive in that when we write a program in BASIC it is done in a sequence of *lines*. Each *line* is given a *line number*, and when we give the program to the computer to run, the instructions that we put in those lines are carried out in order of their line numbers, unless the program that we wrote directs otherwise. (There I go again, throwing you another curve. We computer people will probably never change, always doing things our way.)

GETTING DOWN TO BASIC

This first program that I am going to show you was probably written by someone who wanted to *see* something on a terminal* screen rather than have it blank. The program looks like this:

```
10   REM: This is a dumb dumb program
20   PRINT "Help!! I'm stuck inside this box."
30   GO TO 20
```

Let's examine this program and see what it will do. The first statement starts off with the line number 10, that's simple, but REM must stand for something. It is a REMark. REMarks in BASIC are used to make comments in the program to let other programmers know what we are doing, and to remind ourselves what's going on in any special area of the program. OK! The second statement (line number 20) is a command — PRINT — that tells the computer to print on its communication device or terminal to us the message "Help!! I'm stuck inside this box." The third program statement (line number 30) has the computer, after it is finished with the second command, go back to

---

*A terminal is a type of sending device used to talk to a computer. It will be described further in another chapter.

line 20 and, therefore, repeat the command over again. The result at the terminal would be this:

Help!! I'm stuck inside this box.
Help!! I'm stuck inside this box.
Help!! I'm stuck inside this box.

Over and over and over again.

Now this doesn't seem too exciting, but to the passerby, if he didn't know how to stop the program with a special command, nothing he typed into the terminal would stop the damned thing from printing out "Help!! I'm stuck inside this box" forever. (We will get into those special commands later.) These two commands combined (20 and 30) constitute what we call a loop. Starting with printing "Help!! I'm stuck inside this box" and going back and doing it over again loops us back into a previously done portion of the program.

The reason that the line numbers are increased by 10 is because if we want to add any commands at a later date we have space to put them in. Otherwise, if we used line numbers like 1, 2, 3, we wouldn't have any in between to add things on. (The computer doesn't recognize half numbers like 2-1/2 or 2-3/4).

Let us put the computer to a little more difficult task, like counting from 1 to 20. This program has a few more commands in it, but don't let it scare you. We'll take it a few steps at a time.

```
10   REM: A program to count from 1 to 20
20   PRINT "Type in the number one";
30   INPUT N
```

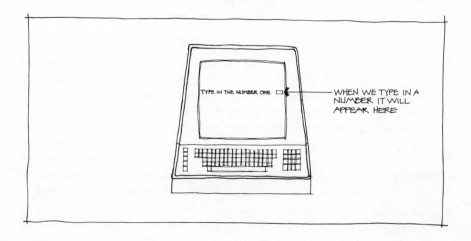

Let's look at the first three steps before we add more. The first command is to give us a remark, the second command will have the computer print out "Type in the number one". This is actually going to be a prompt for the user to respond to. The computer will be asking us a question. The semicolon at the end is a special character that the computer uses to type a response on the same line that it printed the statement.

The next command, "INPUT N", is the response that the user types in (The "N"). It's what the computer will use as data. Oh! By the way, the question mark at the end of the print statement was put there by the computer. It did this automatically because it knows that the user has to type something in and it is the way it asks him to do so.

The significance of the letter N, in the third command, is nothing special; we can use any letter we wish. Let's add a few more statements to the program.

```
40   LET N = N + 1
50   PRINT N
60   IF N < 20 THEN 40
70   PRINT "Finished".
80   End
```

Line 40 gets us into a little bit of math. What I want the computer to do is take the number that the user types in and add a 1 to it, very simple. Here's our friend the PRINT statement again. "PRINT N" will have the computer show us the value of our original input plus 1. Let's push on. In line 60 we come to a very common statement that is used in the programming language BASIC a lot — IF-THEN. The IF-THEN is used in this case to check and see *IF* the number that was typed in at step number 30 plus 1 (that's what we did in step 40, add a 1 to it) is less than (<) 20.   < is a special character that is used to represent "less than". The second part of the statement is *THEN* 40. What I mean is to tell the computer to go back to step 40 and do it again, if the number (N + 1) is less than 20.

This will keep going on until we got to the number 21. Why 21? Because, if we look at the statement in line 60:

```
60   IF N < 20 THEN 40
```

we see that at N + 1 = 21, N is more than 20, and the program moves to the next step, line number 70, which is our friend the PRINT statement. At line 70 the computer will tell us that it is finished. Line 80 lets programmers know we are at the end of our program. Let us put the whole program together and see how it looks.

```
10   REM: A program to count from 1 to 20
20   PRINT "Type in the number one;"
30   INPUT N
40   LET N = N + 1
50   PRINT N
60   IF N < 20 THEN 40
70   PRINT "Finished"
80   End
```

Let's review by drawing out a flowchart (see page 17):

The next illustration shows a flowchart on how we constructed our basic program. When you first start out programming, it pays off to design a flowchart diagram to give you a visual conception of how the program works. You can see the different stages in building the program and its paths to the end.

Let's add a different ending to our program, to jazz it up a little:

```
72   PRINT "If you want to run it again type in Y;"
74   INPUT A
76   IF A = "Y" THEN 20
78   PRINT "Boy! This sure is dumb!"
```

OK! See if you can follow along on this one. Line 72 brings back the PRINT statement asking if we want the computer to run our program again. It will wait for an answer. In 74 we repeat the input routine, using a different letter. 76 is an **IF-THEN** again, but looping us back to the beginning of the program at line 20. Line number 78 is self-explanatory. We'll list the whole program and see how much we have added.

```
10   REM: A PROGRAM TO COUNT FROM 1 TO 20
20   PRINT "Type in the number one";
30   INPUT N
40   LET N = N + 1
50   PRINT N
60   IF N < 20 THEN 40
70   PRINT "Finished"
72   PRINT "If you want to run it again type in Y";
74   INPUT A
76   IF A = "Y" THEN 20
78   PRINT "Boy! This sure is dumb!"
80   End
```

Our forethought pays off when we see the whole program listed. If we hadn't numbered our lines with the spacing of 10 we would not have been able

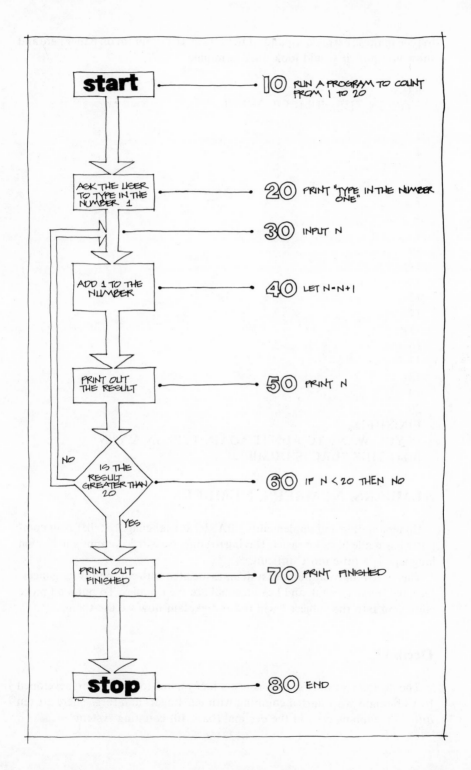

start   10 RUN A PROGRAM TO COUNT
                            FROM 1 TO 20

ASK THE USER   20 PRINT "TYPE IN THE NUMBER
TO TYPE IN THE   ONE"
NUMBER 1

                        30 INPUT N

ADD 1 TO THE   40 LET N=N+1
NUMBER

PRINT OUT   50 PRINT N
THE RESULT

NO
     IS THE   60 IF N < 20 THEN NO
   RESULT
GREATER THAN
     20

        YES

PRINT OUT   70 PRINT FINISHED
FINISHED

stop   80 END

17

to type in these extra commands. OK! I'll run the program on paper here and show you how it would look on a terminal:

```
RUN
TYPE IN THE NUMBER ONE? 1
2
3
4
5
6
7
8
9
10
11
12
13
14
15
16
17
18
19
20
FINISHED
IF YOU WANT TO RUN IT AGAIN TYPE IN A Y? N
BOY! THIS SURE IS DUMB!
```

NUMBERS, NUMBERS, NUMBERS

Understanding and implementing BASIC as a language to talk to our computer has made life a lot easier. Having to converse with a computer in its own language is a little more difficult.

There are four basic number systems associated with computing languages. Decimal, binary, octal, and hexadecimal are their names. To put a bit more confusion into the subject I will try and explain how we use them.

Decimal

The decimal number system is just a fancy name for the system developed by us humans who started counting with our fingers and toes. There are ten different symbols used in the decimal (base 10) counting system:

0123456789

Each column in a decimal number is associated with a different power of 10. For instance in the number 4682, the 2 is representative of a number in the ones column — there are 2 ones. The 8 shows us there are 8 tens; the 6 that there are 6 hundreds; and the 4 that there are 4 thousands. This is nothing new — we have been doing this type of counting all of our lives.

To have the computer recognize the number 4682 in decimal counting plays havoc with its circuits. Remember, the computer only knows "on" or "off", so we must convert the decimal number into something the computer can understand. To do so, binary counting is used.

Binary

In the binary method there are only two symbols:

0 1

This is a base 2 type of system.

You're probably saying to yourself, well how in tarnation with only a zero and a one for symbols can we create the number 4682. Put on your learning cap again (or else!).

Having only two digits, 0 and 1, and creating columns with a base of 2, we can **double** the size of a number each **column** we move over. For instance. within the decimal system, 4682 has a base 10, so we count from *right* to *left* — each column being ten times larger than the one to its right. In binary, each column is two times larger than the one to its right. Thus, for the number 1011, the 1 in the farthest column to the right represents a 1. In the next column the 1 represents a 2 (2 x 1). The next column represents a 4 (2 x 2), and there are none in this number. In the next column, the 1 represents an 8 (2 x 4). The binary number 1011 equals the decimal number 11.

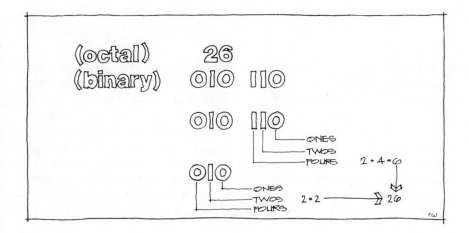

Octal

You have probably guessed that we as humans would have a terrible time if we had to add and subtract or even write in binary code. But don't forget the computer only knows 0 or 1, and with the fantastic microminiaturization process we call microelectronics, the circuits are so small that we are able to store away very large numbers in binary code in a small area.

To help us along a bit we use two additional number systems that have the ability to compact very large binary numbers into a smaller number. The *octal* system has a base of 8, which is just a different power of 2. The symbols used in octal are:

01234567

Let's convert the number 26 (decimal) into an octal number. Having a base 8 and only eight symbols that we can use, we need to divide our decimal number by eight and carry the remainder. Example:

Decimal 26
Divide by 8 ⌐ 26

$$\begin{array}{r} 3 \\ 8 \overline{\smash{\big)}\ 26} \\ \underline{24} \\ 2 \end{array}$$ = remainder (our first digit in octal)

The 2 remainder is our first right-hand digit in the octal conversion. Then we try and divide 8 into our sum number again:

$$\begin{array}{r} 0 \\ 8 \overline{\smash{\big)}\ 3} \\ \underline{0} \\ 3 \end{array}$$ = remainder (our second digit in octal)

Eight won't go into three, so the remainder is three, and that is our next number in our octal conversion. So, converting the decimal number 26 into octal we divide 26 by 8. The result is that 8 can go into 26 three times, with two left over. That's our first digit. Then we divide down again and see if 8 can go into 3; it won't, so 3 is the remainder. Therefore, the decimal 26 is 32 in octal.

But we still have more than a 0 or 1 in octal, so how can octal numbering help us in our computer? Converting octal to binary is a snap. We group three binary digits to represent a single octal number. Since each octal number will never be more than seven, we only need three binary digits. Example:

Let us go back and convert our number 4682 into octal, and then binary

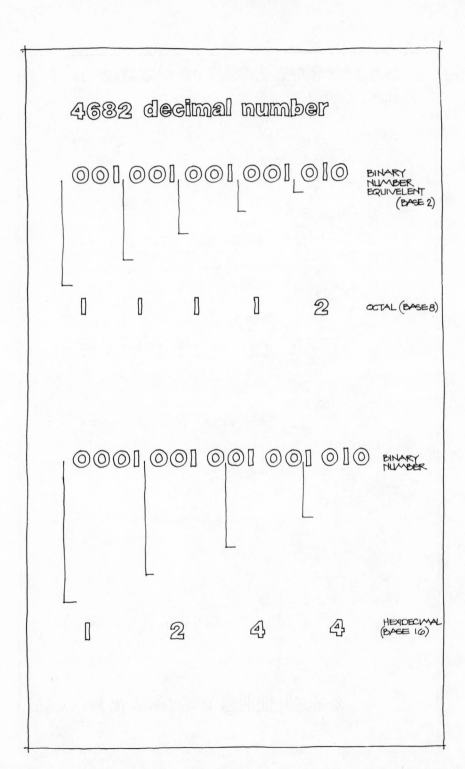

4682 decimal number

001 001 001 001 010   BINARY NUMBER EQUIVELENT (BASE 2)

1   1   1   1   2   OCTAL (BASE 8)

0001 001 001 001 010   BINARY NUMBER

1   2   4   4   HEXIDECIMAL (BASE 16)

converting 4682 in decimal to octal

```
      585
   8│4682
     40
     ──
      68
      64
      ──
      42
      40
      ──
       2  =  │REMAINDER + FIRST DIGIT IN OCTAL│
```

2

```
       73
    8│585
      56
      ──
      25
      24
      ──
       1  =  │REMAINDER + SECOND DIGIT IN OCTAL│
```

12

```
       9
    8│73
      72
      ──
       1  =  │REMAINDER + THIRD DIGIT IN OCTAL│
```

112

```
       1
    8│9
      8
      ──
      1  =  │REMAINDER + FOURTH DIGIT IN OCTAL│
```

1112

```
       0
    8│1
      0
      ──
      1  =  │REMAINDER + FIFTH DIGIT IN OCTAL│
```

11112

octal 11112 = 4682 decimal

octal. Decimal 4682 is 11112 in octal.

Here is our octal number back into binary.

(OCTAL)	1	1	1	1	2
(BINARY)	001	001	001	001	010

Hexadecimal

With a base of 16, hexadecimal has sixteen different symbols we can use:

0123456789ABCDEF

Zero through 9 are the same as in decimal numbering. We add the letters A through F to represent the numbers 10 through 15, respectively.

In converting a decimal number to octal we use 8 as our base to divide by. In hexadecimal we use the base of 16, the same way. Example: Let's convert our decimal number 4682 into hexadecimal (see page 24).

Let's review all four number systems (see page 25).

The only reason that I put you through this agony was to show you how the computer "reads" the basic decimal numbering system.

If you didn't understand what was going on, don't be alarmed. It isn't really necessary to be able to convert back and forth between these types of systems. The computer can do it without you, but it must do so to break down our decimal numbers for internal use as zero's (off) or one's (on).

PROGRAMMING SINCE THE DARK AGES

During the evolution of the computer (in the 1950's), the programmer evolved from the engineer who designed the machine and made it work to a very specialized person who plays with one's and zero's. In the early days, the programmer was actually a technician of sorts, involved in altering the physical structure of the machine. It was the programmer's job to make changes that would have the effect of giving the computer instructions or tasks to do. The early computers were more or less single-task machines with single programs. What I mean is that a computer was developed and built to handle one job, and the program to do that job was the only program ever used.

As the computing machinery developed and became more sophisticated so did the programming. Instead of conversing with the computer in its language, which was called (for obvious reasons) *machine language,* a more highly developed language was developed, *assembly language.*

This type of computing language was one step up from machine language in

converting 4682 in decimal to hexidecimal

```
        292
    16 | 4682
        32
        ___
        148
        144
        ___
         42
         32
         ___
         10  =  | REMAINDER + FIRST DIGIT IN HEX |
```

10 or A

```
        18
    16 | 292
        16
        ___
        132
        128
        ___
          4  =  | REMAINDER + SECOND DIGIT IN HEX |
```

4 A

```
         1
    16 | 18
        16
        ___
         2  =  | REMAINDER + THIRD DIGIT IN HEX |
```

24 A

```
         0
    16 | 1
         0
        ___
         1  =  | REMAINDER + FOURTH DIGIT IN HEX |
```

124 A

1248 hex = 4682 decimal.

in decimal numbering

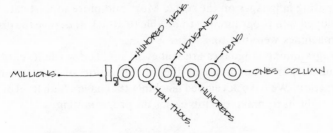

MILLIONS — 1,000,000 — ONES COLUMN
HUNDRED THOUS. — THOUSANDS — TENS
TEN THOUS. — HUNDREDS

in **binary** numbering

ETC. 64's 32's 16's EIGHTS FOURS TWOS
1000000 · ONES

4682 in decimal

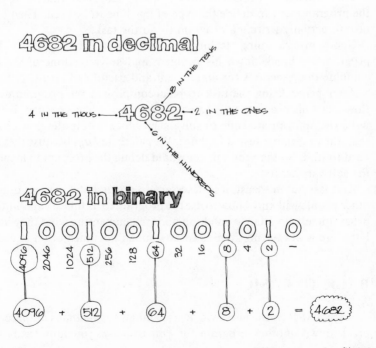

4 IN THE THOUS. — 4682 — 2 IN THE ONES
6 IN THE TENS
6 IN THE HUNDREDS

4682 in **binary**

1 0 0 1 0 0 1 0 0 1 0 1 0
4096 2046 1024 512 256 128 64 32 16 8 4 2 1

4096 + 512 + 64 + 8 + 2 = 4682

that the assembler would now do some of the more menial programming tasks that required a tremendous amount of time and were very repetitious. You were still at a very basic level of programming, though.

The evolution of bigger and better computers brought an influx of computing languages on the scene. More and more sophistication had to be developed into programming to be able to attack and solve the problems that the machines were put to.

Programming languages are still evolving. Today the level of computing languages has brought about the simplification of the human/computer interaction. We have developed machines that have a high level of intelligence built right in to make the job easier on programming.

CHART THE PROGRAM'S FLOW

The methods of teaching programming have not actually changed. Programmers are still taught that the first thing to be done is to define the program or task to be accomplished. The next is to determine the input structure, or how data is to get into the machine, and what that data is made up of. On the other side is how and what data should look like when it comes out of the machine. From determining what goes in and what has to come out, the programmer can define the type of machine to be used. Then comes the task of actually writing a program to do the task.

Good programming techniques have been developed to help the programmer break down his problem and solve sections of the task and combine these sections for an efficient and useful end result.

After generalizing the task to be accomplished the programmer should flow-chart his program to get an overall view of what is needed. He will then write the appropriate code to solve each block within the flow chart. After that, the program is tested for bugs. We call them *bugs* because they are often hard to find. So the programmer would debug the program to locate and fix the software errors.

And last but not least, it is necessary to document what was done so that other people will know how to use the program to its fullest capabilities. Most programmers do a fairly good job about documenting what they have done, but there is always no limit as to how much documentation is needed.

BACK TO BASIC

Since BASIC is the most widely used language in home computers, we will break down another program for you to show you how easily it can be understood and used.

This chapter is only meant to be a highlight into programming, showing you, the home computer owner, how not to be afraid of it! Later in the Reference section I will list other books that delve deeper into the subject.

The program that we will break down for you is a game called NUMBER GUESS. The way the game is played is the computer will think of a number between 1 and 100. It is your task to guess that number. The computer will keep score as to how many guesses you make. The object is to guess the number the computer is thinking of in the fewest of guesses. The computer will give you clues along the way by telling you if your guess is either too high or too low from its number.

The first thing we will do is flowchart the start of the program. The best way to break down and understand how a program works is to follow a flowchart. So let's look at the first few steps in the program.

In the start circle we will put or REMark line numbers to let others know a few particulars about our program:

```
10  REM:  THE COMPUTER CHOOSES A NUMBER FROM
20  REM:  1 to 100 AT RANDOM, THE OBJECT OF
30  REM:  THE GAME IS TO GUESS THE CHOSEN
40  REM:  NUMBER IN AS FEW GUESSES AS POSSIBLE
```

Lines 10 through 40 will give a brief explanation of the function of our program. The next block gets us into a function of the BASIC language that we call library functions. Library functions are preprogrammed steps in BASIC that will do things automatically for us. We don't have to tell the computer how to do them, we just give a command and it will generate a result. Line number 50 is:

```
50  LET R = 1 + INT (100*RND)
```

Breaking this statement down will show two library functions: INT and RND.

With the LET statement, we want the computer to set a value to a specific variable. The significance of the letter R doesn't matter, we can use any letter we want. The rest of the statement is a little tougher.

$$1 + INT (100*RND)$$

The INT function stands for integer. What this will do is to truncate or round off a number to its nearest whole. If a number is 2.35, for instance, INT will round off the number to 2. If the number is 2.73 it will round off the number to 3. The statement before INT is 1 +; what we are going to do is add a one (1) to the integer number that we generate. The next part of the statement (100*RND) is put into parenthesis because we want to separate the library functions in BASIC so the computer will understand them a little easier.

RND stands for random. This function will generate a random number between 0 and 1. Depending on how the BASIC that you are using was written, the random number that is generated can vary in how many places beyond the decimal point it goes. For instance the number could be .2385647, which would be seven places, or .9143, which would be only four.

Anyway, RND will generate a number from zero to one. The asterisk symbol * stands for multiplication in BASIC. So we want the computer to multiply 100 times the random number generated. Let's review the whole line number.

$$50 \quad \text{LET R} = 1 + \text{INT} (100*\text{RND})$$

We are asking the computer to set a value to R. We are saying add a one to an integer, or rounded off number, that is 100 times a random number. Let's say the random number generation chooses the number .5634, which multiplied by 100 becomes 56.34. Truncated or rounded off to the closest whole, 56.34 becomes 56. 56 plus 1 = 57. Thus the number 57 is assigned as the value to R. R is the number we are trying to guess.

The next block in our flow diagram is setting the guess counter to zero. What this part of the program will do is keep track of how many guesses it took us to find the number. Line 60 reads:

$$60 \quad \text{LET Y} = 0$$

At this point we are telling the computer that there have been zero attempts at guessing the number.

The next block is what we will print out on the terminal to the user; what the object of the program is:

```
 70   PRINT "A RANDOM NUMBER HAS BEEN"
 80   PRINT "PICKED BY THE COMPUTER. TRY"
 90   PRINT "AND GUESS IT. HINT! THE NUMBER"
100   PRINT "IS FROM 1 TO 100. GOOD LUCK!!"
110   PRINT
```

Wait a minute, there must be a typo because line 110 just says PRINT and there is nothing to print. A PRINT statement with nothing following shows that we wish to skip a line.

The next block is our prompt to the user to input their guess.

```
120   PRINT "YOUR GUESS IS =";
130   INPUT X
```

In the other program we used the semicolon at the end of the PRINT statement so that the terminal would print our input on the same line. Input X is our statement to the computer for our guess. Let's stop here and list what we have so far.

```
10   REM: THE COMPUTER CHOOSES A NUMBER FROM
20   REM: 1 to 100 AT RANDOM, THE OBJECT OF
30   REM: THE GAME IS TO GUESS THE CHOSEN
40   REM: NUMBER IN AS FEW GUESSES AS POSSIBLE
50   LET R = 1 + INT (100*RND)
60   LET Y = 0
70   PRINT "A RANDOM NUMBER HAS BEEN"
80   PRINT "PICKED BY THE COMPUTER. TRY"
90   PRINT "AND GUESS IT. HINT! THE NUMBER"
100  PRINT "IS FROM 1 TO 100. GOOD LUCK!!"
110  PRINT
120  PRINT "YOUR GUESS IS =";
130  INPUT X
```

I hope you have followed along so far. If not, go back and look over the flow chart. Let's add some more building blocks to our flow chart.

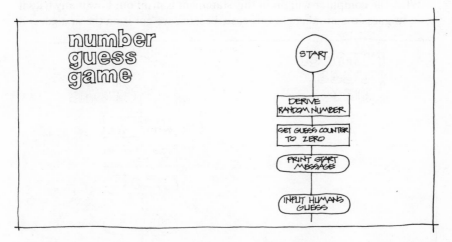

Line 140 is straightforward. Back in line 60 we set the guess counter at zero because there hadn't been any input yet. In line 140:

140   LET Y = Y + 1

We now have an input from our user, so the variable Y is equal to 1 at this point.

Our next block, X = R, is an IF-THEN statement:

150   IF X = R THEN 180

What we are going to do here is compare the random number the computer has generated with the input guess from the user. We are stating *IF* X, which is the user guess, is equal to R, the computer random number, **THEN** go to another step. At this point, if we evaluate that the two numbers are equal we take the yes side of the block, if not we take one of the no side. We will start with the yes side.

We will skip over lines 160 and 170 at this point to go to 180. The reason this is done is because in BASIC the computer follows each line number in sequence, so it is easier to jump over some steps to allow the computer and the programmer to follow the program more easily. On the yes side we have added the block:

180   PRINT "NOT BAD!! — YOU GOT IT!!!!"

We now can add more line numbers to follow and continue the yes side:

190   PRINT "YOUR NUMBER OF TRIES WERE"; Y

What the computer will do in this statement is print out how many tries it took to guess the number. In this case, because we got it on the first guess it

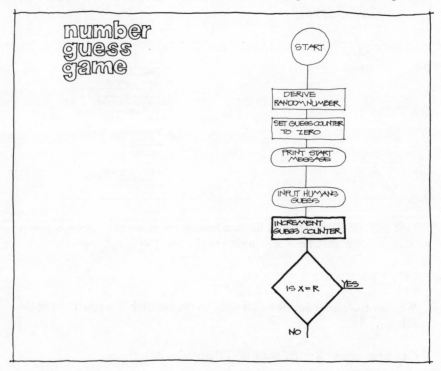

only took 1. The next block is asking if we want to play again.

```
200   PRINT
210   PRINT "IF YOU WANT TO TRY AGAIN TYPE IN Y"
220   PRINT "IF NOT TYPE IN AN N";
230   INPUT L
240   IF L = Y THEN 50
250   STOP
```

Line 200 is our "skip a line PRINT statement." Lines 210 and 220 are asking if we want to play again. Input L in line 230 is our input to the question. Line 240 will evaluate our input and take the appropriate action. If the answer is a Y then the computer would go back to line 50 and start the program all over again. If N is the response, then the program would be over. We will list the program again and show you where we are:

```
10    REM: THE COMPUTER CHOOSES A NUMBER FROM
20    REM: 1 TO 100 AT RANDOM, THE OBJECT OF
30    REM: THE GAME IS TO GUESS THE CHOSEN
40    REM: NUMBER IN AS FEW GUESSES AS POSSIBLE
50    LET R = 1 + INT (100*RND)
60    LET Y = 0
70    PRINT "A RANDOM NUMBER HAS BEEN"
80    PRINT "PICKED BY THE COMPUTER. TRY"
90    PRINT "AND GUESS IT. HINT! THE NUMBER"
100   PRINT "IS FROM 1 TO 100. GOOD LUCK!!"
110   PRINT
120   PRINT "YOUR GUESS IS =";
130   INPUT X
140   LET Y = Y + 1
150   IF X = R THEN 180
160
170
180   PRINT "NOT BAD!! — YOU GOT IT!!!!"
190   PRINT "YOUR NUMBER OF TRIES WERE"; Y
200   PRINT
210   PRINT "IF YOU WANT TO TRY AGAIN TYPE IN Y"
220   PRINT "IF NOT TYPE IN AN N";
230   INPUT L
240   IF L = Y THEN 50
250   STOP
```

Now we can go back and fill in lines 160 and 170.

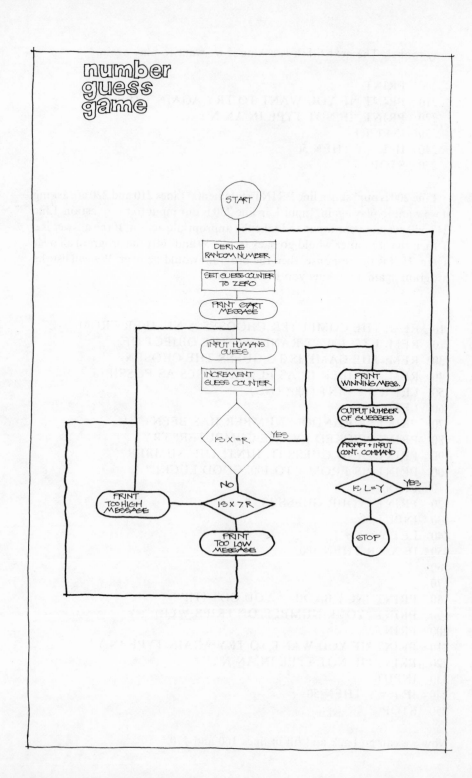

Now we are going to look at the no side of the block that was asking if our random number equals our guess. In line 150, the yes side took us to the finish of our program and also asked us if we wanted to play again. If the statement was false or if the random number didn't equal the guess, we would then progress to line 160:

```
160   IF X  <  R THEN 260
```

In this statement we are comparing two numbers again. The computer will compare our guess, X, and see if it is greater than (<) R, the random number. If it is we would go to line 260. If it is not we would then progress to line 170. As an example, let's say that it was greater than R. Line 260 would read:

```
260   PRINT "TOO HIGH, TRY AGAIN"
270   GO TO 120
```

The computer is giving a line to the user that the guess they put in is higher than the computer's random number. So the computer would loop back to line 120 and have the user put in another guess.

If the guess, X, is not greater than R, the random number, we would progress to line 170.

```
170   GO TO 280
```

This statement would have us go to the statement that printed the opposite of greater than:

```
280   PRINT "TOO LOW, TRY AGAIN"
290   GO TO 120
```

In either case, if the guess was either too high or too low the computer would let the user know and loop back to have them try again.

Now that we have looped back to line 120 again, the computer would continue as before and print out "YOUR GUESS IS =";, and the user would type in another guess. At this point the program has been altered a bit. As the program progressed in line 140, the statement was LET Y = Y + 1. Since we have already made one attempt at guessing the number, Y is equal to 1. So our second guess would change the value of Y to 2 in step 140.

This process of asking questions and comparing the results will be done over and over again until the user guesses the number. All the while the computer is keeping score of how many guesses. Let's list the whole program:

```
10   REM: THE COMPUTER CHOOSES A NUMBER FROM
20   REM: 1 TO 100 AT RANDOM, THE OBJECT OF
30   REM: THE GAME IS TO GUESS THE CHOSEN
40   REM: NUMBER IN AS FEW GUESSES AS POSSIBLE
50   LET R = 1 + INT (100*RND)
60   LET Y = 0
70   PRINT "A RANDOM NUMBER HAS BEEN"
80   PRINT "PICKED BY THE COMPUTER. TRY"
90   PRINT "AND GUESS IT. HINT! THE NUMBER"
100  PRINT "IS FROM 1 TO 100. GOOD LUCK!!"
110  PRINT
120  PRINT "YOUR GUESS IS =";
130  INPUT X
140  LET Y = Y + 1
150  IF X = R THEN 180
160  IF X = R THEN 260
170  GO TO 120
180  PRINT "NOT BAD!! — YOU GOT IT!!!!"
190  PRINT "YOUR NUMBER OF TRIES WERE"; Y
200  PRINT
210  PRINT "IF YOU WANT TO TRY AGAIN TYPE IN Y"
220  PRINT "IF NOT TYPE IN AN N";
230  INPUT L
240  IF L = Y THEN 50
250  STOP
260  PRINT "TOO HIGH, TRY AGAIN"
270  GO TO 120
280  PRINT "TOO LOW, TRY AGAIN"
290  GO TO 120
300  END
```

One more thing line 300 tells us: it's the end of the program and there are no more line numbers to follow. We computer people sometimes forget there is an end to something!

To summarize, I hope this chapter has given you a little insight into how we talk to a computer through different languages. By no means does it give a complete description of the language BASIC. In the last chapter I have listed a few books that you might read to give you a little more knowledge.

IV.

THE BEST HARDWARE
BUZZWORDS

Now that we have gone through the basics of how we talk to personal computers, we will next deal with the equipment itself. *Hardware* refers to the parts of a computer system we can actually put our hands on. Much like a stereo system, a computer system is made up of different modules or parts. In a basic stereo system you need a tuner, receiver, amplifiers, and speakers. Each working independently cannot produce music, but all working together will give you the desired result.

Of course, when we talk basics in any system we can always make it bigger and better. You can add things like cassette decks and turntables to have your stereo system do more. In a computer system we can do the same thing.

First of all I need to define the terms we will be dealing with. So put your training hat back on and I will go through some basic hardware terms.

CIRCUIT BOARD = A

special board on which specific circuits have been etched, or "printed." The basic material is a thin sheet of insulating material that a layer of copper has been bonded to, then a layer of tin goes on next. By using a photographic technique areas of the tin and copper are etched away, leaving thin lines called traces.

Motherboard

MOTHERBOARD = A printed

circuit board with a specific bus structure that many different kinds of printed circuit boards can be plugged into.

BUS = A wire that carries an

electrical signal to two or more printed circuit boards. A bus structure would be many bus lines that carry many different signals.

Bus

MICRO, MICROCOMPUTER, MICROPROCESSOR=
These terms mean the same as the CPU. "Micro" came into being when we learned to make things small. The circuit itself is about the size of a pencil eraser.

CPU= The Central Processing Unit is the brain of the computer, the part of the computer that thinks.

RAM= Random Access Memory: temporary storage used by your computer to allow you to change the data you have put into it, which is then transferred to a mass storage device.

ROM = Read Only Memory. This is memory also, but it has been programmed to give out the same kind of information all the time. It never forgets and cannot be changed.

EPROM = Much like ROM, EPROM (Erasable Programmable Read Only Memory) does not forget but has one added feature. You can erase the information that you have programmed in it by using an ultraviolet light and reprogram with different information.

INTERFACE or **I/O** = A connector that "translates" between two parts of a system. You generally need one interface for each peripheral that you hook to your computer.

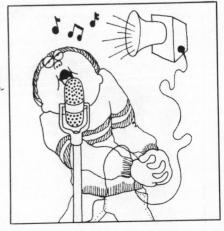

38

SERIAL I/O: This type of interface transmits and receives data to and from the CPU through a single stream of electrical signals. Serial transmission is used when the requirements to hook up the peripherals to your CPU must travel through low-quality long distance channels.

PARALLEL I/O: This type of interface transmits and receives data on a batch mode, where there are several signals interchanged at the same time. These kinds of transfers can happen very fast, but can't be sent too far.

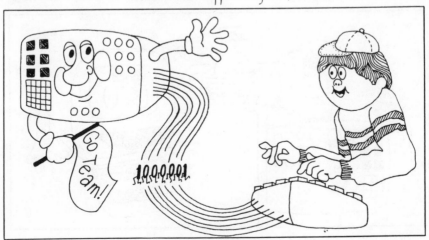

BUFFER = This is a holding area for information to equalize or balance two different operating speeds. For example, the output of the computer might be too fast for a printer, so the information would be held in a buffer until the printer could accept the next batch of data to be printed.

PERIPHERALS = The devices attached to your computer, such as the <u>display</u>, keyboard, printer, etc.

MASS STORAGE:
Any way of keeping a lot of information **OUTSIDE** your computer, but available to it. This is your computer's "memory." Most common kinds of mass storage are <u>tape</u> and <u>disk</u>.

CASSETTE STORAGE:
In a personal computer we can use an ordinary auto cassette player to store information through a special interface.

FLOPPY DISK:
A mass storage device that uses a flexible platter to store a large amount of information.

HARD DISK = Much like a floppy, a hard disk *stores* a tremendous amount of information, but its platter is much larger and not so portable.

TERMINAL = A unit for conversing (input or output) with your computer. It has a keyboard, plus display or print-out.

TVT = "Television typewriter." A keyboard and electronics specially designed to turn your TV into a terminal.

CRT = Your computer's "TV screen," showing you what's IN there. The CRT (cathode-ray tube) is your computer's way of talking to you. It is also referred to as a display unit or terminal.

BUG: The cause of a malfunction, usually in a program. They're called "bugs" because they can be hard to find.

V.

WHAT MAKES UP A COMPUTER AND HOW IT WORKS

You are probably saying to yourself, "OK! I got through the first few pages without too many problems and I like the cartoons, but now we get to the heavy stuff." Don't worry! In this chapter I am going to try and make learning as painless as possible. I won't deal with the super technical stuff — just a very simple explanation of what it takes in hardware to make up a personal computer. By hardware, I mean the physical things we can touch, the actual equipment.

In addition, I will explain the inner workings of these magic boxes, how you communicate with your computer, and how it is able to communicate with you.

All digital computers operate in basically the same way. Computer differences are created by the different uses the machines are put to. The larger and more complicated the job, the larger and more complicated the computer.

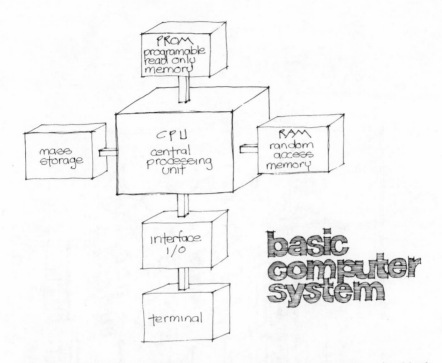

The first illustration in this chapter, The Basic Computer System, is a block diagram of the modules that make up the simplest digital computer. Each block represents a group of circuit components. We will describe now each of the modules and what its role is, and show you how they interact.

THE CENTRAL PROCESSING UNIT (CPU)

The first and most important module is the CPU or **CENTRAL PROCESSING UNIT.** This is the brain of a computing system. The CPU does all the actual work: calculation, data comparison, data alteration, and data reception and transmission.

There are a wide variety of CPU's on the marketplace. Depending on whom you talk to, one is always better than the other. Don't let this confuse you now. All you really need to know is that all CPU's function basically the same. We will get into the particular types later.

The CPU, which is sometimes called the controller, is an LSI circuit. Large Scale Integration (LSI) is the process of putting thousands of components in a very small area. To give you an example, using LSI technology, a dot this size, ., could contain over 1000 transistors. Hard to believe, but true. Being able to reduce the physical size of the components required to do the job has made it

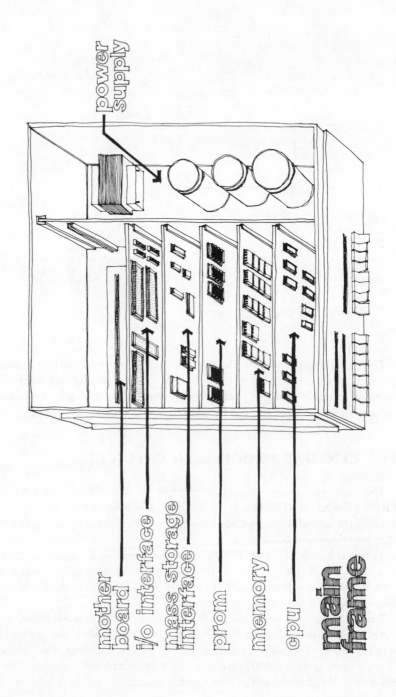

power supply

mother board

i/o interface

mass storage interface

prom

memory

cpu

main frame

possible for us to do the same type of computing work in desk-top microcomputers that it took a large room full of vacuum tubes to do 20 years ago.

The CPU acts much like a receiver-amplifier in a stereo component system. Your stereo collects radio signals through an antenna and its receiver decipers those signals, puts them in some kind of order, and sends them to the amplifier section. The amplifier boosts them up and transmits them to your speakers, where they are outputted as sound. Your amplifier can also receive signals from other devices as well — turntables and tape decks provide stored signals that are processed and outputted. The CPU, too, collects or calls in signals (data) from different modules, acts on them and outputs signals through the same or other modules.

RAM

RANDOM ACCESS MEMORY is the module in a computer system that is the *temporary* storage device for programs and data for the CPU to process. This storage device keeps all the instructions, and data for those instructions, in an orderly fashion so that the processor can act on them.

Memory is organized much like the sorting boxes in a post office. Each memory location can hold (or store) a fixed amount of information. In a

micro, each memory location can store one byte or eight bits. They also are numbered so the CPU can find them quickly and are labeled by an "address" (a sort of name).

This type of memory, RAM, is *volatile,* which means the information stored in each memory location can be changed or erased. RAM requires that power be applied all the time. When the power to the machine is turned off, the RAM forgets what is stored inside it (its memory is erased) and it has to be taught all over again.

Remember from Chapter III on programming that those memory locations or addresses play a very important part. The processor is the HEART of the computer system BUT the RAM is the organizer. It sets up the CPU so the data can be processed, much like you would take a recipe for a cake and follow the instructions for baking it.

ROM

READ ONLY MEMORY stores information just like RAM does, but it has one property that RAM does not, *IT NEVER FORGETS.* Even when the power is turned off, it will still remember what is stored inside.

This type of module gives us a fantastic tool that we use constantly. In the programming chapter we mentioned that the basic computer system itself can not do anything until we give it a list of instructions. We also mentioned that there was a list of those instructions that had to be used all the time. These are stored in ROM. Thus, ROM allows us to store important, often-used instructions, so we don't have to keep inputting them, time and time again.

In all microprocessor-based home computers the total amount of random access memory, or RAM, that the CPU can access is 65,536 bytes. We break that down and put in address (or number) associated with each byte. Starting with the logical number 0 we then number each location in a hex address* up to the maximum, 65,536.

It is not necessary to have 65,536 bytes of memory in your home computer all at once. In fact, you as an individual home computer owner would never need that much. I only mention it to let you know the limitations of the microprocessor-based machines.

MASS STORAGE — RAM ON THE RUN

The mass storage module allows us to store a tremendous amount of data outside the computer. It is our active file cabinet, so to speak. Paper tape,

---

*If you don't remember hex numbering, go back to Chapter III, Programming, and review.

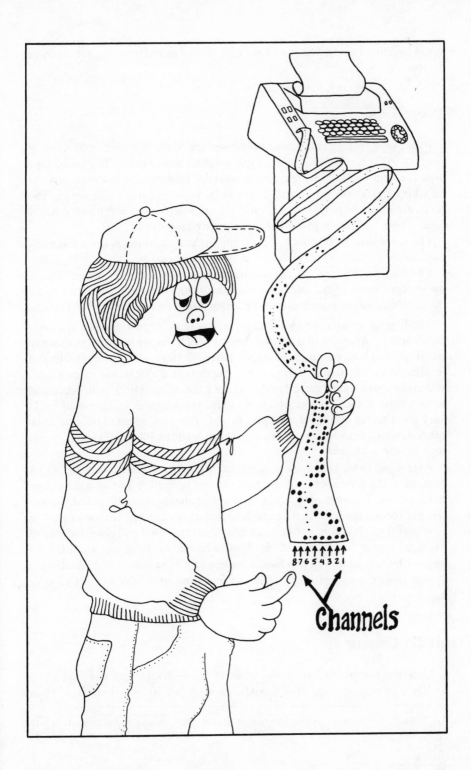

Channels

audio cassette, floppy disk, and hard disk are the most common mass storage devices.

Paper Tape

Paper tape storage is the most primitive type of storage used in computing systems. As it is still used today, I feel we need to discuss it. The paper tape used is a thin one-inch wide continuous strip. Information is stored on it by punching holes into the paper. These holes represent one's and zero's. The holes are punched in eight horizontal columns across the width of the paper tape. These eight hole positions are called "channels".

The combination of punched and unpunched positions in these channels constitutes the ASCII code that you read about earlier.

The data pnched (or stored) on the tapes can be read, or loaded, with a *paper tape reader.* When the tape is driven through the reader, it will translate the combination of punched and unpunched holes back to the ASCII code.

The biggest disadvantage of a paper tape system for storing information is the enormous quantity of it needed. Ten rows of holes are punched per inch of paper tape. Thus, one inch of paper tape will store only ten characters of information. A further disadvantage of paper tape is that it takes a long time, relatively speaking, to record and read back the information on it. Read and write times, or the speed at which the holes are punched and are read back, vary from ten to 100 characters per second. This might seem fast, but when other devices are available that can do this job 100 to 1000 times faster, paper tape becomes obsolete.

Regarding time, you must understand that when you are working with a computer, the time spent waiting between one operation and another can be burdensome if it adds up quickly. You are probably thinking, "Ten characters per second is very fast; that's 600 characters per minute. Nobody can even type that fast." It is true nobody can type that fast, but if you consider that an average "basic interpreter"* is 8000 characters long, it would take approximately 14 minutes to load it from paper tape into RAM. And if the system does not accept it correctly the first time, you have to start all over again.

Audio Cassette

In home computers, an audio cassette is the least expensive and most widely used mass storage device. Audio cassettes are 10 to 15 times faster than

---

*A "basic interpreter" is the language that we use in a computer system for conversing.

paper tape, so they are tremendous time savers.

Storing data on an audio cassette is quite simple. Audio recording techniques have made it possible for us to generate frequency tones that shift very rapidly. The fact that the computer only recognizes one's and zero's works greatly to our advantage using such tones. By convention, a tone of approximately 1200 cycles per second represents a zero and a tone of approximately 2400 cycles per second represents a one. These tone shifts, or zero's and one's, can be set to a pattern that the computer will be able to "read".

Using integrated circuits, engineers have designed a printed circuit board interface that can generate or decipher these shifting tones at the speed of 100 to 150 bytes per second. Unlike paper tape, which deciphers all seven bits of a word at one time, audio cassettes do it in a serial stream. One bit at a time is recorded on the tape. Paper tape can record ten bytes or computer words per inch of tape; audio cassette recording uses one inch of tape to record 100 bytes of data.

The main disadvantage of audio cassette recording for mass storage is the reliability of the recorder and also the tape itself. After using a very inexpensive home tape recorder over a period of time, the motors and recording head start to wear and you will not get a very good transfer of data. All it takes is one byte missing in the wrong place, and all of your data could be bad. Also, the tape used will stretch and the data would be wrong.

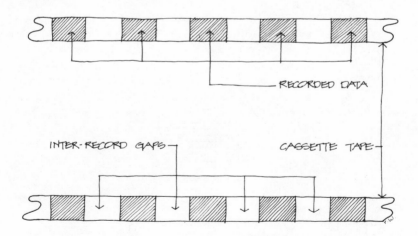

Floppy Disk

Floppy disk data recording is the most advantageous to use in home computing. It gives you both speed and reliability when recording and retrieving information, but it is the most expensive of the three.

A floppy disk looks like a 45 RPM record made of a very thin plastic, much like audio cassette tape. It is kept in an envelope that protects the disk from damage and keeps it rigid.

Recording on a floppy disk is done by the same serial technique as on audio cassette. Though it does not use an audio tone, it records the data by a digital signal one bit at a time. Using a read/write sensor head, the floppy disk drive mechanism comes in contact with the floppy disk and will record data by tracks. These tracks have been numbered so that when we want to retrieve the information that has been stored we will be able to locate that information very quickly.

Hard Disk

Much like floppy disks, hard disks record and retrieve data the same way. By using sections on the disk pack we can compact a tremendous amount of data in a small area.

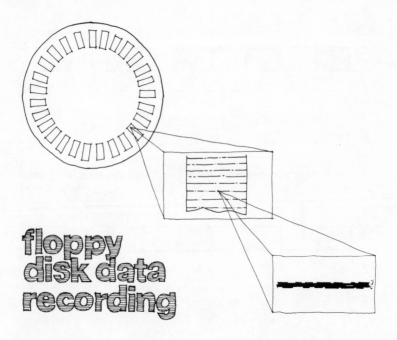

floppy disk data recording

Hard disk record storage is done by using a read/write head which makes contact with the disk pack. The speed at which the disk turns and the size of the disk make the hard disk able to store ten to fifteen times the data than a floppy disk can.

I/O OR INTERFACE

To get into the CPU in a way useful to us humans, we need input/output devices, which connect to the CPU through interfaces. The interfaces are electronic circuits that permit controlled data flow from the CPU and its memory components to us on the outside at our various terminals. Our input/output devices, of course, are the keyboards and CRT's or printers we use to exchange information with the CPU.

There are two basic I/O interfaces used in home computing: serial and parallel.

Serial Interface

Serial interface is widely used because it is the easiest to use. In the basic hook-up only three wires are needed: transmit data, receive data, and ground.

The serial I/O takes the ASCII code, or the seven bits, and sends and receives that data one bit at a time. The serial I/O is used where your computer system is linked to outside peripherals over a long distance. (The distance limitation is dependent usually on how the interface and the peripheral are constructed, either current loop or RS232. Both of these types of serial interface are used.)

Parallel Interface

Parallel I/O is a little more difficult to hook up than serial I/O. Parallel types of interfacing require all the data bits to be connected at one time, so you usually have nine or ten wires going between the computer and the peripheral devices. You have lines for the seven data bits that make up the ASCII letter or number, a ground line, and one or two lines that we call "hand-shake" lines. These hand-shake signals communicate back and forth information between the peripheral and the computer. This information lets the peripheral know when the computer is ready to accept another character and vice versa.

This type of data transfer is done on a *batch mode,* in which the entire byte or word is transferred at once. This type of I/O is used when you want to have a very fast data transfer. Its drawback is that the computer cannot be very far away from the peripheral.

TERMINALS

A standard microcomputer terminal looks like a TV screen with a typewriter keyboard hooked on to it. This is the peripheral device that we use to communicate with the CPU. It is our link to the computer so we are able to give it the necessary instructions to do a job and the data or food it wants to fill those instructions.

There are any number of ways that these terminals are made up. First there is the stand-alone terminal; a typewriter-like keyboard, CRT (cathode ray tube) or TV monitor, and all the electronics necessary to generate the ASCII code alphanumerics.

Other video display units have been introduced into the marketplace as well. These modules are printed circuit boards that have been developed to reside inside the computer system. By hooking up a keyboard for input and a monitor or modified television set for output, you have a terminal. This method has been adapted by the home computer market because it is cheaper to manufacture and can cost less for the consumer.

Other types of terminal devices sold today combine the keyboard with a hard copy or paper output. Hard copy output provides you with one advantage over the CRT terminals: a permanent record exists of the conversation between you and the computer. This is a definite advantage in some cases. Most of the time, however, your conversation does not have to be

recorded for posterity. The main disadvantage of using a hard copy terminal is the constant replacement of paper and ink ribbons. Also, these types of terminal are a mechanical device, and the moving parts for printing will wear down quickly and have to be replaced periodically.

In comparison, the CRT display is quiet and fast. Its disadvantage, of course, is not having a permanent record, but you can hook up a printer to your home computer. The hard copy type gives you the permanent record, but is very slow.

PRINTERS

When using a CRT, it is desirable from time to time to keep a permanent record of the transactions between you and your computer. Again there are different types of printers available. Their cost varies according to the speed at which they print and the quality of print.

Dot matrix printers are the lowest in cost and usually the fastest. Letter quality printers which are actually typewriters that have been developed for high speed and constant use are more expensive.

SINGLE BOARD COMPUTERS

Up to now I have been discussing the different modules that make up a

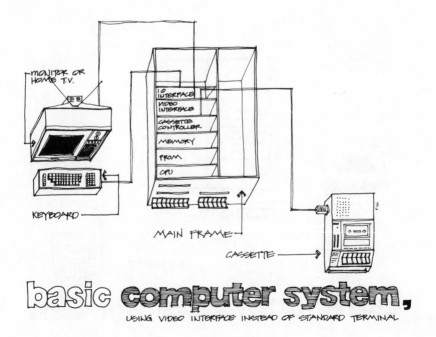

MONITOR OR HOME T.V.

I/O INTERFACE
VIDEO INTERFACE
CASSETTE CONTROLLER
MEMORY
PROM
CPU

KEYBOARD

MAIN FRAME

CASSETTE

basic computer system,

USING VIDEO INTERFACE INSTEAD OF STANDARD TERMINAL

microcomputer system as individual printed circuit boards. But in this advanced age of electronics we have compacted all of these individual modules onto one single card.

These single board computers, as illustrated in the next caption, have all the components it takes to make up a home computer. The advantage, of course, is that using a single card requires less space, also less power, so it can be compacted into a smaller box which saves money, both to the manufacturer and to the consumer. The disadvantage is in not using the standardized bus structure; the consumer has to wait until the particular manufacturer whose computer he just purchased brings to market add-on peripherals such as printers, floppy disks, tape readers, etc.

Using the home computer bus standard, labeled the S-100 bus, consumers have the advantage of shopping from a tremendous variety of boards and peripherals that are on the marketplace today. Buying an S-100 bus computer gives the home computer buyer the advantage of purchasing from dozens of manufacturers, rather than just one.

THE MAIN FRAME BONE'S CONNECTED TO THE CRT BONE

The illustrations on these pages show some of the more common ways that

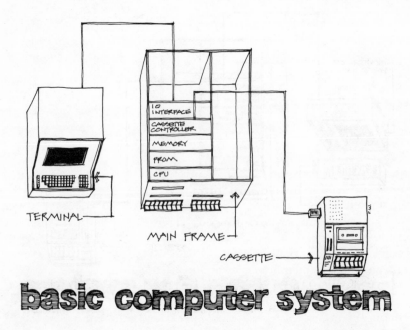

TERMINAL

IO INTERFACE
CASSETTE CONTROLLER
MEMORY
PROM
CPU

MAIN FRAME

CASSETTE

basic computer system

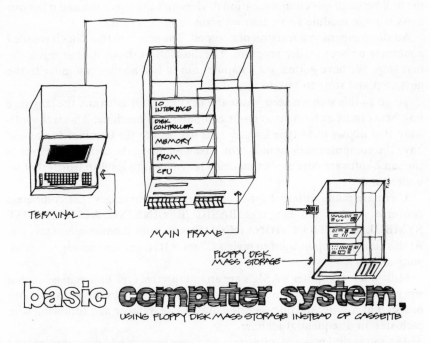

basic computer system,
USING FLOPPY DISK MASS STORAGE INSTEAD OF CASSETTE

Labels in figure: TERMINAL, MAIN FRAME, FLOPPY DISK MASS STORAGE, IO INTERFACE, DISK CONTROLLER, MEMORY, PROM, CPU

home computers have been hooked up. As you can see there are a number of ways that a home computer can be put together. But it is necessary that all of the components are there to make the whole thing work. As you get more exotic and want faster response time and don't want to wait too long in between program loadings, the cost of the system can and will go up.

TO TIE IT ALL TOGETHER,
PLUG IN SOFTWARE

As we discussed in the programming chapter, there are two basic types of software: systems and applications. We also told you about the often-used systems instructions, usually located in ROM, that are necessary to get the computer going.

Waking up a computer system is much like probing a human into getting out of bed in the morning. After turning on the power, it is usually required to hit some sort of reset button. What this does is clear the CPU's head, so to speak, and focus its attention on a specific memory location, which initiates the start-up routine. This is done by our old friend ROM. The program or list of instructions that is in ROM does a number of things. First it opens one of the doors or ports in the CPU so it can do our calculations for us. It also opens the link between our communication devices and the computer and it lets our mass storage module know that we want to look into it.

All this happens in a fraction of a second. The program that does it is called a monitor or boot loader program. The illustration shows us that this is the first step. We have gotten our computer out of bed and we can move to the next step and start to talk to it.

To go to this step we need to use the next block of software, the language link between us as humans and our computer as a machine. This is the software that allows us to type English type words into the terminal device and have the computer understand them. Likewise, when the computer responds the same software converts its machine language into English words that we understand.

There are many different types of higher level languages that computers converse in, but the language BASIC **(BEGINNING ALL-PURPOSE SYMBOLIC INSTRUCTIONAL CODE)** is what most home computers use. At this time you might want to review Chapter III on programming to refresh your memory.

Most home computer BASICs are an interpretive type of language, in that when we write a program or list of instructions, it follows those instructions one step at a time, starting with the lowest line number and following with each step in a sequential manner.

As soon as the language software is active we can move to our next step: our

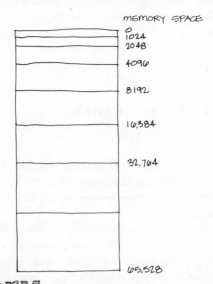

MEMORY SPACE
0
1024
2048
4096
8192
16,384
32,764
65,528

memory
address breakdown.

application program itself. The application program is the actual project that we have for our computer system to work on.

Within the application program we will give the computer system a chance to ask for data by asking the computer operator questions. The operator will then feed in the data requested by the computer.

Let us review this sequence once more. First, the power goes on and we hit some sort of reset. This clears the computer's head, opens a port to the CPU, sets up the link between the peripheral terminal and the computer, and tells the mass storage device that we want to transfer a program or data into the memory bank.

Then we load the language BASIC into memory. This is done basically three different ways. If the computer system has BASIC loaded in ROM, you would tell the computer that you wanted it accessed into memory by giving it an address to go to. In some machines you would type just one character; others require more information. If the home computer system has BASIC in ROM, it is usually very simple to transfer it into memory.

Home computers that use audio cassettes to load BASIC are almost as simple. In the monitor program, there is a list of instructions to the CPU that translates the different frequency shifts to one's and zero's. As these instructions are already in ROM usually all that is required is to type in "load", or "get BASIC", and then turn on the recorder to play.

memory usage

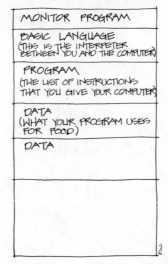

| MONITOR PROGRAM |
| BASIC LANGUAGE (THIS IS THE INTERPRETER BETWEEN YOU AND THE COMPUTER) |
| PROGRAM (THE LIST OF INSTRUCTIONS THAT YOU GIVE YOUR COMPUTER) |
| DATA (WHAT YOUR PROGRAM USES FOR FOOD) |
| DATA |

HOW YOUR MEMORY IS USED UP

1.

2.

3.

4. Applications Program

Checkers

Basic Language

5. Data

Floppy disks are not as fast as loading in BASIC from ROM, which just takes a fraction of a second, but are much faster than audio cassette or paper tape. You would usually just type in "go BASIC" or "basic" or "get BASIC", and the computer would search the disk to find it, and then load it into memory.

After BASIC is in the memory bank, we would then either load or type in an application program and run it. During the course of the program, you would interact with the computer, answering the questions it asks, or asking it questions.

VI.

HOW IT WORKS

We are going to take you back now to that eventful day when Willy interviewed his computer. Through the graces of his pen and tape recorder, here is that fateful conversation.

Willy:	Good morning, Computer!
Computer:	Good morning, Willy. Did you sleep well?
Willy:	Yes! Pretty good. How about yourself?
Computer:	My circuits are rested. What would you like me to do for you today?
Willy:	Well, actually I want to know how you work. What I mean is, what makes you tick?
Computer:	This is an unusual request. Usually you want to play Star Trek, or checkers, or balance your checkbook. What gives?
Willy:	I don't know. The guy who created me is making me ask you these questions. I guess he needs to learn something.

Computer:	He's supposed to be the expert.
Willy:	Yeah, I know. But we might as well do what he says, or he might draw a different set of clothes on me. I really don't want that; I was just getting used to these.
Computer:	OK! Ask away.
Willy:	What I've learned so far about you is that you are made up of modules. Is that right?
Computer:	You're right. I have many different parts that make up my whole, just like yourself.
Willy:	The CPU, RAM, ROM, I/O, and peripherals are those modules. What we really want to know is how each of these things work.

CPU CIRCUITS

Computer:	OK, let's start off with my brain. The CPU or **Central Processing Unit,** has groups of circuits within it that do all my thinking.
Willy:	What are those circuits called?
Computer:	Not so fast, let's take this one step at a time. Now, do you remember what my CPU is doing for you?
Willy:	I *think* so. Doesn't it carry out commands?
Computer:	That's right! You have a program that carries out instructions.
Willy:	One step at a time, like baking a cake?
Computer:	Yes. If my CPU is going to get those commands or instructions from memory, it must have some way of knowing where to go to get the instructions.
Willy:	Something to keep track of where in the program it is, right?
Computer:	Exactly. My CPU needs to have some place to store those memory locations. It's called the **Program Counter.** Memory locations inside my CPU are called registers, so the program counter is a 16-bit register.
Willy:	Wait a minute. I thought that a computer word was seven bits, with an eighth bit for parity.
Computer:	You're right. But don't you remember that those memory locations had an address, a sort of name?

Willy:	Yes.
Computer:	Well, that name is a 16-bit word that forms that address. The data inside that location is the ASCII word. That 16-bit word is a hex address which the program counter can access very quickly. Willy, I think you need a little review. Go back a few days and review Programming, please!
Willy:	Don't get smart, or I'll turn you off.
Computer:	I'm sorry, where were we. Oh, yes! Anyway, we have a program counter that finds those instructions and brings them in one at a time. Now, when my CPU receives the next step in the program from memory, it has to save it somewhere until it figures out the instruction. So I have another register called the *Instruction Register* that stores the command that the CPU is currently working on. Since my CPU has to decode or figure out these instructions, it needs another part to do that, so we have another part called the *Instruction Decoder and Control Unit.*
Willy:	What does the CPU do with the instruction it got from memory and put into its instruction register?
Computer:	This instruction is decoded within the CPU and triggers a microprogram that is permanently stored in the CPU. The result is a series of control signals sent out by a control unit causing various events to occur, which finally cause the result you asked for in the eight bits of the machine-code instruction.
Willy:	Are you saying that every instruction I write causes a stored program within the CPU to be executed?
Computer:	Now you've got it.
Willy:	Do I have to write the microprograms stored in the CPU?
Computer:	No, they are usually permanently stored in the CPU when it is manufactured. The microprograms are written by the engineers who designed the chip.
Willy:	Why do you say "usually?"
Computer:	I didn't think you'd notice that. Some CPU's called "bit-slice chips" let the user write the microprograms, so they can design their own computer's instruction set; but that's too advanced for this conversation. Maybe we'll talk about that in another book.
Willy:	Boy, I knew this was going to be tough.
Computer:	Not really. Let's look at what we have: The three parts we

have so far are *the program counter,* which points to the instructions and brings them in, *the instruction register,* which stores the command the CPU is currently working on, and *the decoder and control unit,* which figures out the commands.

Willy: This isn't so tough.

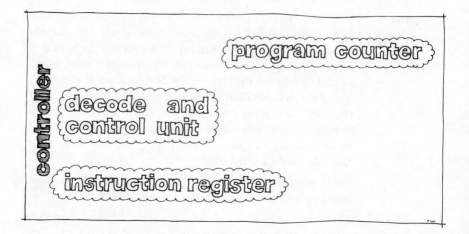

Computer: OK, Willy, let's look at the other parts. We also have an *address buffer,* which stores the next piece of data for processing by the decoder and control unit.

Willy: Wait, I thought that the program counter did that.

Computer: No, the program counter stores the addresses or names of the memory locations. The address buffer stores the address of data that is in it. A buffer is the same thing as a register, we just call it a different name.

Willy: OK.

Computer: Another thing the CPU has to do is to do some math calculations, and along with that we need a place to store the answers when it gets done. This section we call the *accumulator.*

Willy: Why doesn't the CPU just send the answer back into memory and give us the answer?

Computer: Well, Willy, because if the next command that was coming into the CPU had to do with the answer that it just figured out, it wouldn't be there. Also, if the CPU wanted to send it back into memory, it would have to know where to send it.

So you would have to have another address register as part of the CPU.

Willy: It gets a little complicated in there, doesn't it?

Computer: Right! Let's just say that they designed it that way.

Willy: Fair enough!

Computer: OK, now let's examine what else we have added to my CPU. Another thing there is a *status flag register* that stores the information about the most recent result of the accumulator so the control unit can do something with it.

Willy: How many more modules?

Computer: Just one. The whole thing is tied into a *clock.*

Willy: You can't tell me that there is a wristwatch in there, too!

Computer: No, but something like it. Having all those commands running around in there can get kind of confusing, so we provide a timer which keeps everything coordinated and working properly.

Willy: OK, I think I understand what's going on. But what about those people who got utterly confused as soon as you opened your mouth, or circuits?

Computer: Let's not get personal, Willy, I'm only a machine. Let us review.

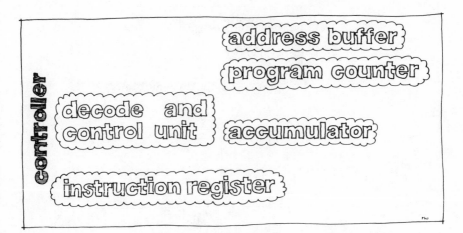

Willy: Well! I guess your brain has been pretty well scattered all over.

Computer: Unlike you, Willy, I can be back together.

Willy: Enough funny stuff. Let's push on. What's next?

WHEN IS A BUSS NOT A BUS?

Computer: All you ever wanted to know about busses but were afraid to ask.

Willy: Enough, already.

Computer: Sorry! I couldn't help that one.

Willy: Is a buss a form of transportation?

Computer: Hey, that's good. In a way, yes. A buss is a set of wires carrying signals used by the computer to perform similar jobs. I hope you remember that by a signal we mean a voltage level indicating a 0 or a 1 that can be used by circuits we call logic gates to make certain things happen.

Willy: Seems to me that a buss is more like streets running parallel to each other, carrying information rather than automobiles. Have I got it right?

Computer: Yes, you're doing fine.

Willy: What kinds of busses will I see in a computer?

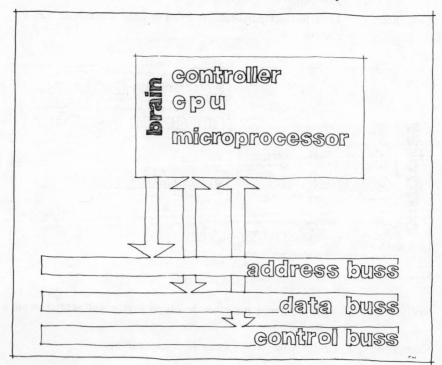

Computer:	There are different kinds. In a typical computer we need busses to serve as communication paths between the building blocks that make up a computer system. You need an address buss so that information goes back and forth to the correct parts of the computer. Then you need a data buss to send bits of information back and forth and finally you need a control buss. The control buss is used to send special signals needed to cause events to happen at the correct time, for instance reading or writing data to or from memory.
Willy:	Are those the only kinds of busses I will see?
Computer:	No, there are a variety of special busses to do specific jobs. For instance there are busses used to connect a computer to laboratory instruments; for instance a device being used to measure radiation from a gas in a chemistry lab. We also have special busses designed to facilitate high-speed data communications.
Willy:	You told me a buss is a collection of signal lines. Does that mean that all computer designers lay out these wires the same way?
Computer:	No, they don't, and that's unfortunate, because it makes it hard for people who design boards to go into a computer since they have to take into account how the buss is constructed in the computer they want to design their board for.
Willy:	Seems to me that could cause a lot of confusion. Why couldn't people get together and decide once and for all how to lay out those wires?
Computer:	You're awfully clever today. What I said before is generally the case, but we're very fortunate in that there is one standard buss used by a lot of hobby computers, especially those using the 8080 CPU.
Willy:	Does it have a name, so that I'll recognize it when I see it?
Computer:	Yes. It's a collection of 100 signals, not all of which are used today, and not all of which are used by any single board. It was first used in the MITS Altair computer and then by the IMSAI. Some people call it the S-100 buss and others chose to call it the hobbyist Standard Buss. There have been meetings held by hobbyists to standardize use of this buss and to assign uses to some of the presently unused lines for the future. Things are not quite as rosy as I've pictured them, because a few of the 100 lines have been used by different designers for different functions, and that could cause a few conflicts.

Willy:	Hey, I've got a thought. Could you ever use one of the buss lines for more than one purpose and not get into trouble?
Computer:	You're almost getting too smart for me. The answer is yes. In some cases if you're trying to save the number of lines needed, you can use a buss line for one purpose at one time in the computer cycle and at another time use if for a different purpose. Of course, you would need some gate circuits to steer each signal to the right place. They even give this technique a fancy name — multiplexing. But let's stick to our S-100 buss, which doesn't use multiplexing.
Willy:	Is the S-100 buss described somewhere?
Computer:	Yes, in several hobby magazine articles, and just for you we'll put one in an appendix to this book.
Willy:	You mentioned an address buss, a data buss, and a control buss. What are they?
Computer:	The address buss has 16 lines, since most microcomputers can address 65,536 memory locations (remember 2^{16} = 65,536, but in computerese we call that 64K). Since the word of information for most microcomputers contains eight bits of information, the data buss has eight lines. By the way, since you would never be sending data in two directions at the same time, you could use those eight data lines in what we call a bidirectional mode. That is, for data out from the CPU to the rest of the computer, or going the other way to the CPU. However, the S-100 buss people decided to use eight lines for data out and eight separate lines for data in.
	As far as the control buss goes, you basically need some 5 to 12 signals to run a microcomputer system. For the S-100 buss, since they wanted to be very flexible, there are many more control lines. I don't want to confuse you now, but when you get to know a bit more about the computer you can look up the details for yourself. By the way, although I didn't mention it specifically, the S-100 buss also has power and ground lines with power at various voltages needed by different kinds of devices you may want to connect to the computer.
Willy:	Where are all those 100 buss lines you talk about?
Computer:	Well, they are all laid out in a prescribed set-up on something we call a back-plane or motherboard. The 100 lines are brought out to a standard 100 pin edge connector. Some motherboards have up to 22 identical edge connectors avail-

Technical Book LIST

ELECTRONICS

Author	Title	Price
Ainslie	Practical Electronic project building	2.60
Aldridge	Transistorised Radio Control for Models	3.50
Amos	Radio TV and Audio Techical Reference	30.70
Amos	Principles of Transistor Circuits	5.50
Ashe	Electronics Self Taught	4.40
Ashe	Handbook of IC Circuit Projects	2.30
Badmateff	How to build Speaker Enclosures	3.90
Bishop	Electronic Projects in the Home	2.75
Bell	Radio Valve and Semiconductor data	3.45
Bognor	Introduction to Digital Filtering	10.35
Brown	How to read electronic circuit diagrams	4.10
Brown	Sixty Four Hobby Projects for Home and Car	2.10
Brown	Questions & Answers on HI-FI	1.90
Brown	Questions & Answers on Transistors	1.90
Brown	Questions & Answers on Electronics	1.90
Buckwater	Easy Speaker Projects	3.30
Burr Brown	Designing with Operational Amplifiers	16.65
Burr Brown	Function Circuits design and applications	15.95
Burr Brown	Applications of Operational Amplifiers	8.30
Burr Brown	Operational Amplifiers Design and Applications (Tobey)	7.40
Capel	How to build electronic kits	2.20
Capel	Microphones in Action	3.00
Capel	Improving your HI-FI	3.50
Capel	Creative Tape recording	4.00
Carlson	Communication Systems, Intro to Signals & Noise	7.50
Carr	FM/Stereo Quad Receiver Servicing Manual	1.80
Carr	Op. Amp. Circuit Design and Application	4.00
Carson	Simplifier Computer programming	2.20
Clayton	Linear Integrated Circuit Applications	5.40
Clayton	Operational Amplifiers, 2nd edition	10.00
Clayton	Experiments with Operational Amplifiers	3.40
Clifford	Microphones — How they work & How to use them	4.85
Clifford	Modern Electronic Maths	6.50
Clifford	Test Instruments for Electronics	2.10
Cohen	Hi-Fi Loudspeakers and Enclosures	9.45
Coker	Questions and Answers on Electric Motors	1.90
Colin	Programming for Microprocessors	8.45
Colwell	Electronic Diagrams	2.60
Colwell	Electronic Components	2.60
Colwell	Printed circuit assembly	2.60
Colwell	Project planning and building	2.60
Crowhurst	Basic Audio Systems	1.90
Crowhurst	Basic electronics course	6.30
Cunningham	Understanding and Using your VOM and VTM	1.80
Darr	New ways to diagnose electronic troubles	1.70
Darr	How to test almost everything electronic	3.50
Drake	Radio controlled helicopter models	3.95
Earl	Audio Technicians Bench Manual	3.50
Earl	Pickups and loudspeakers	3.50
Earl	Tuners and Amplifiers	3.00
Earl	Cassette Tape Recorders	5.25
Earl	ABC of Hi-Fi	4.25
Everest	Acoustic techniques for the home and studio	1.70
Flind	Electronic Projects in Music	2.75
Flynn	MOS Digital IC's	5.10
Fox	Practical Triac/SCR Projects for the Experimenter	2.25
Gaddis	Trouble-shooting solid state amplifiers	1.90
Gardner	Tape recorder servicing manual Vol. I	9.10
	Vol. II	9.10
George	Electronic Projects in the Car	2.75
Graf	Build-it Book of Safety Electronics	3.65
Graf	Build-it Book of Home Electronics	3.65
Graham	Simple Circuit Building	2.60
Green	RTTY Handbook	2.60
Green	Practical Test instruments you can build	2.10
Green	Solid state projects for the experimenter	2.10
Greenfield	Practical digital design using IC's	12.70
Gilbert	Advanced applications for pocket calculators	4.20
Goddis	Trouble-shooting solid state wave generating and shaping circuits	1.80
Goodman	Indexed guide to modern electronic circuits	2.30
Guilou	Beginners guide to Electric Wiring	3.35

Author	Title	Price
Hallmark	Electronic measurements simplified	2.00
Hallmark	Microelectronics	3.90
Haviland	Built-it of miniature test & measurement instruments	4.10
Herrington	How to read Schematic Diagrams	4.70
Hellyer	Questions and Answers on Radio and TV	1.90
Hellyer	Tape recorders	4.25
Hibberd	Questions and Answers on Integrated Circuits	1.90
Horowitz	How to troubleshoot and repair electronic test equipment	2.70
Hudson	Colour television Theory	7.10
Hunter	CMOS Databook	5.45
Jackson	Questions and Answers on Electricity	1.90
Jeffries	Radio Control for Model Yachts	1.85
Kennedy	Electronic Communications Systems	8.50
King	Beginners guide to radio	3.35
King	Beginners guide to Television	3.35
King	Beginners guide to Colour Television	3.35
King	Colour television servicing	8.40
King	Master Hi-fi installation	3.45
King	FM radio servicing handbook	5.45
King	Rapid servicing of transistor equipment	4.45
King	Radio, television and audio test instruments	6.80
King	Audio handbook	7.50
King	Servicing with the oscilloscope	6.50
Kitchen	Handtools for Electronic workshop	2.75
Kitchen	Electronic Test Equipment	5.20
Klein	Introduction to Medical Electronics	2.00
Kyle	Electronics unravelled	1.90
Lancaster	Incredible Secret Money Machine	4.95
Mandz	Electronic puzzles and games	2.20
Mannassewitsch	Frequency Synthesis	23.40
Margolis	10 minute test techniques for PC servicing	1.90
Marston	110 COSMOS Digital IC Projects for the Home Constructor	3.95
Marston	110 Waveform Projects for the Home Constructor	3.95
Marston	110 Operational Amplifier projects for the Home Constructor	3.95
Marston	110 Semiconductor projects for the Home Constructor	3.95
Marston	110 Thyristor/SCR projects for the Home Constructor	3.95
Marston	110 Electronic Alarm projects for the Home Constructor	3.95
Marston	110 Integrated Circuit projects for the Home Constructor	3.95
Marston	20 Solid State projects for the Car and Garage	3.20
Marston	20 Solid State projects for the Home	3.20
Melen	Understanding CMOS Integrated circuits	4.00
Master	Transistor/Integrated Circuit Substitution Handbook	6.20
Melen	Understanding CMOS Integrated Circuits	4.00
Miller	Questions & Answers on Electric Wiring	1.90
Milman	Integrated electronics	7.90
Morris	Essential formulae for electrical and electronic engineers	1.65
Morris	Digital electronic circuits and systems	3.50
Penfold	Electronic Projects in Audio	2.75
Penfold	Electronic Projects in the Workshop	2.75
Price	Homeowners guide to saving energy	4.85
Rabiner	Theory and applications digital signal processing	23.80
Rayer	Electronic Projects in Hobbies	2.75
Rayer	Electronic Game Projects	2.75
Reddihough	Questions & Answers on Colour Television	1.90
Safford	Radio Control Manual	2.45
Salm	Tape recording for fun and profit	2.00
Sands	Mobile radio handbook	1.70
Saunders	Working with the oscilloscope	4.00
Saunders	Working with semiconductors	1.70
Scroggie	Foundations of wireless and electronics	5.00
Seissons	Stereo Quad hi-fi principles and projects	1.60
Sehunaman	How to test instruments in electronic servicing	2.10
Sinclair	Introducing Amateur Electronics	1.55
Sinclair	Introducing Electronic Systems	1.80
Sinclair	Electronic Fault Diagnosis	3.45
Sinclair	Repairing pocket transistor radios	2.50
Sinclair	The Oscilloscope in Use	3.00
Sinclair	Understanding electronic components	4.25
Sinclair	Understanding electronic circuits	4.25
Sinclair	Audio Amplifiers for the Home Constructor	2.75
Sinclair	Beginners guide to Tape Recording	3.35
Sinclair	Beginners guide to Integrated Circuits	3.35
Sinclair	Beginners guide to Audio	3.35
Smith	Basic electronic problems solved	1.90
Stapleton	Beginners Guide to Computer Logic	1.90
Steckler	Simple transistor projects for hobbyists	1.70

Author	Title	Price
Streater	How to Use IC Logic Circuit Elements	3.65
Swearer	Installing and servicing electronic protective systems	1.90
Swearer	Pulse switching circuits	2.20
TAB Staff	Popular Valve/Transistor Substitution Guide	2.10
Taub	Principles of Communication Systems	8.10
Texas Instruments	Transistor Circuit Design	9.35
Texas Instruments	Designing with TTL Integrated Circuits	9.05
Towers	Practical Solid State DC Supplies	6.20
Towers	International FET Selector	4.35
Towers	International Transistor Selector	10.20
Towers	International Op. Amp. Linear IC Selector	7.50
Towers	Semiconductor Circuit Elements	7.40
Tuite	Practical Circuit Design for the Experimenter	2.60
Turner	125 One Transistor Projects	2.10
Turner	ABC's of FET's	3.70
Turner	Electronic Engineers Reference Book	34.00
	Transistor Tabelle	4.10
Wanniger	Using Electronic Testers for Car Tune Up	1.80
Wakerly	Logic Design Projects Using Standard IC's	5.10
Ward	Solid State Circuit Guide Book	2.25
Ward	Computer Technicians Handbook	7.75
Waters	ABC's of Electronics	4.25
Weis	How to Repair Musical Instrument Amplifiers	2.50
Wells	Fire and Theft Security Systems	1.90
Wells	Transistor Circuit Guidebook	4.00
Wells	Transistor Circuit Guidebook	4.00
Wells	Computer Circuits	4.85
Wilding	Solid State Colour TV Circuits	7.30
Wilding	TV Technicians Bench Manual	5.10

MINICOMPUTER − MICROPROCESSOR BOOKS

Author	Title	Price
WHAT IS A MICROPROCESSOR − Book and Two Casettes		12.00
Adams, C.	Beginners Guide to Computers and Microprocessors with projects	5.60
Ahl,	Basic Computer Games	5.25
Albrecht, B.	Basic for Home Computers	5.30
Albrecht, B.	Basic − A Self teaching guide 2nd edition	5.30
Alcock, D.	Illustrating Basic	2.60
Arnold, R.	Modern Data Processing	6.60
Aspinall, D.	Introduction to Microprocessors	6.40
Altman, L.	Microprocessors	10.65
Altman, L.	Applying Microprocessors	12.00
Barden, W.	Z80 Microcomputer Handbook	7.65
Barden, W.	How to Buy and Use Mini-computers and Microcomputers	7.75
Barden, W.	How to program Microcomputers	7.00
Barna, A.	Introduction to Microcomputers and Microprocessors	8.15
Bibbero, R.J.	Microprocessors in Instruments and Control	12.45
Boyle, J.	Digital Computer Fundamentals	12.85
Bursky, D.	Microcomputer Board Data Manual	5.40
Bursky, D.	Microprocessors Data	5.40
Clifton, H.	Business Data Systems	6.00
Coan, J.S.	Basic Basic	7.50
Coan, J.S.	Advanced Basic	5.80
Dijkstra. E.	Discipline of Programming	15.10
Ditlea,	A Simple Guide to Home Computers	4.00
Duncan	Microprocessor Programming & Software Development	13.85
Freiberger, S.	Consumers Guide to Personal Computing and Microcomputers	5.50
Frenzel, L.	Getting Acquainted with Microprocessors	7.10
Fry, T.	Computer Appreciation	3.95
Fry, T.	Further Computer Appreciation	4.95
Gilmore, C.M.	Beginners Guide to Microprocessors	4.75
Gosling, R.E.	Beginning Basic	3.25
Graham, N.	Microprocessor Programming for the Computer Hobbyist	7.00
Grosswirth	Beginners Guide to Home Computers	3.10
Hanson, P.	Operating System Principles	16.30
Hanson, P.	Architecture of Concurrent Programs	16.00
Hartley,	Introduction to Basic	2.40
Haviland, N.P.	The Compulator Book	6.20
Heiserman, D.L.	Miniprocessors from Calculators to Computers	4.85
Hilburn, J.L.	Microcomputers, Microprocessors, Hardware, Software and Applications	16.95
Hill, F.	Digital Systems, Hardware Organisation, Design	9.00

Author	Title	Price
Huggins, E.	Microprocessors and Microcomputers	5.45
Jong, W.	IC Op. Amp. Cookbook	10.00
Jong, W.	IC Timer Cookbook	7.50
Jong, W.	IC Converter Cookbook	9.50
Kemeny, E.G.	Basic Programming	6.65
Klingman, E.	Microprocessor Systems Design	16.95
Korn, G.A.	Microprocessor and Small Digital Computer Systems for Engineers and Scientists	21.40
Larsen	Logic Memory Experiments using TTL IC's	8.15
Lancaster, D.	TV Typewriter Cookbook	7.75
Lancaster, D.	Cheap Video Cookbook	6.50
Lancaster, D.	TTL Cookbook	7.00
Lancaster, D.	RTL Cookbook	4.65
Lancaster, D.	CMOS Cookbook	8.20
Lancaster, D.	The Incredible Secret Money Machine	4.95
Lesea, A.	Microprocessor Interfacing Techniques	8.50
Leventhal	Introduction to Microprocessors	16.70
Libes, S.	Small Computer Systems Handbook	5.75
Lippiatt	Architecture of Small COmputer Systems	4.35
Loofbourrow	How to Build a Computer COntrolled Robot	5.30
Lewis, T.G.	Mind Appliance Home Computer Applications	4.75
Martin, J.	Principles of Data Based Management	16.50
Martin, J.	Computer Data Base Organisation	20.00
Martin, J.	Security-Accuracy & Privacy in Computer Systems	20.85
Martin, J.	Design of Man-Computer Dialogues	19.00
Martin, J.	System Analysis for Data Transmission	22.60
Martin, J.	Telecommunications and the Computer	22.30
Martin, J.	Design of Real-Time Computer Systems	16.50
Martin, J.	Programming Real-Time Computer Systems	13.85
McGlynn, D.R.	Microprocessors — Technology, Architecture and Applications	9.00
McMurran	Programming Microprocessors	5.50
Motil, T.	Digital System Fundamentals	7.60
Moody, R.	First Book of Microcomputers	3.85
Monro	Interactive Computing with Basic	3.65
NCR	Basic Electronics Course with experiments	7.50
NCR	Data Processing concepts course	6.30
Nagin, P.	Basic with Style	4.00
Ogdin, P.H.	Software Design for Microcomputers	7.00
Ogdin, P.H.	Microcomputer Design	7.05
Peatman, J.B.	Microcomputer Based Design	20.40
Peatman, J.	Design of Digital Systems	7.90
Peckham	Basic: A Hands-on Method	6.85
Peckham	Hands-on with a Pet	8.70
Rao, G.U.	Microprocessors and Microprocessors Systems	20.50
Rosen, A.	Word Processing	11.50
Rony, P.H.	The 8080A Bugbook: Microcomputer Interfacing and Programming	7.60
Rony,	Introductory Experiments in Digital Electronics and 8080A Microcomputer Programming and Interfacing	10.50
Scelbi	6800 Software Gourmet Guide and Cookbook	8.80
Scelbi	8080 Software Gourmet Guide and Cookbook	8.80
Scelbi	Understanding Microcomputers	8.60
Soucek	Microprocessors and Microcomputers	19.00
Schoman	The Basic Workbook	3.70
Sirion, D.	Basic from the Ground Up	6.00
Spracklen, D.	Sargon	9.75
Spencer	Game Playing with Basic	4.70
Spencer	Computers in Society	3.80
Titus	8080/8085 Software Design	7.45
Titus	Microcomputer Analog Converter	7.45
Tracton	57 Practical Programs and Games in Basic	6.40
Veronis	Microprocessor	12.85
Waite	Your Own Computer	1.80
Waite, M.	Microcomputer Primer	6.25
Ward	Microprocessor/Microprogramming Handbook	6.00
Wirth	Systematic Programming	12.75
Wirth, N.	Algorithms+Data Structure=Programs	16.20
Zaks, R.	Introduction to Personal and Business Computing	8.50
Zaks, R.	Microprocessors from Chips to Systems	8.50

able for connection. If you have a printed-circuit board you want to connect, all you have to do is bring the lines you want connected out to projecting fingers on the bottom edge of the board and insert it into the motherboard and, voila, you are off and running. The last time I counted there were some 600 boards made by over 100 manufacturers and any one of these can be plugged into any available slot on the S-100 buss board.

Willy: Well, now that you've told me something about the CPU, which does all the thinking, and the busses, which are used to transmit information in the form of voltage levels that correspond to zero's and one's, what are we going to talk about next? What about memory? That's the place where the computer stores all those bytes you've talked about that are the program and data the computer needs to make it do something, isn't it?

Computer: You're absolutely right on. Memory is the first thing we should talk about in the world of the computer that lies outside of the CPU. But before we do, I think I should mention something that applies generally to all of the devices we want to connect to the various busses we just discussed. It didn't seem to bother you, but there's a problem we have to solve straight off. What's going to happen if we connect many devices to the same buss lines? Off-hand, you'd think chaos would arise if every device was to think it was in control of the buss at the same time. We handle this by using what we call tri-state devices. We normally think that the state of every pin on a chip is either logic level 0 (0-.8 volts) or logic level 1 (2.0-5 volts). A third state exists for our tri-state devices. We call it the high-impedance state. That's an engineer's fancy word to say that he has effectively completely disconnected the chip from the buss. So you see, to prevent any conflicts, all we have to do is see that every device connected to the buss is in the high impedance state except for the one we want to be in control. I hope you keep that in mind from now on in all our conversations.

Willy: Whew! That was sure a mouthful. I think I got it. All devices have to be the fancy kind, what you call it . . . oh, tri-state. Is that true?

Computer: Well, not quite, but I didn't want to confuse you. We also have open-collector devices that use a transistor at the output so that when the device is off the signal line is pulled high to 5V (a 1). And when the device is on the line, it is pulled down to 0V (a 0). You have to be careful how you connect several of them at the same time. Even when they are off, they draw some power and you might need a large power supply if you used all open-collector devices. Why don't we forget about them now because we will use tri-state devices most of the time anyhow.

Willy: OK. Can we talk about memory now?

Computer: Sure, what do you want to know?

Willy: I hardly know where to start. For beginners, what do we need memory for?

IT'S IMPORTANT TO HAVE A GOOD MEMORY

Computer: Thanks for starting off with an easy one. We need memory to store eight-bit binary words that, when properly interpreted by the CPU, can represent programs, data, characters to be output to a printer or other device, and a host of other things.

Willy: What does memory look like?

Computer: For the most part like any other IC. They are large-scale integrated circuits with a good deal of hardware on a small chip.

Willy: Is there just one kind of memory chip, then?

Computer: I wish it were that easy. They come in many sizes and what's more there are quite a few varieties. We're going to have to talk about RAM's, ROM's, PROM's, and EPROM's, for starters.

Willy: Whew! It sounds like Greek to me. Do those letters stand for something like IRS and NCAA?

Computer: They sure do. For instance, RAM stands for **Random Access Memory.** I'm a little sorry we started these, since all the memory I'm talking about now is random access. By that I mean you can get to the word you want without having to search from the beginning until you come to the one you want. We should really call RAM "Read-Write Memory," which means that you can read what is inside such as characters or data, and also change or write into it as well.

Willy: Is all RAM alike then?

Computer:	The world's not that simple. RAM can either be static or dynamic. Static memory will retain its data as long as the power to the chip is on. On the other hand, dynamic memory stores its data in a lot of tiny capacitors and the voltage of these capacitors leak with time. This means that somehow you must rewrite the data back to each memory location or it's gone forever. Luckily the process of reading a dynamic memory cell will rewrite the data. We call this a refresh cycle, and the dynamic memory chip must be refreshed about every two milliseconds. A clever designer can arrange to have this done by special hardware circuits on the memory board which read the chip at a time in the cycle when no one else needs the address buss. Done this way it doesn't slow down the processor and you are not even aware of it happening. In computer jargon we call it a transparent refresh cycle. Some CPU's are even smart enough to do the refresh for you at the right time in the cycle so that again it doesn't slow the CPU down.
Willy:	OK, static or dynamic, I guess the next question is how many words are stored in a single memory chip.
Computer:	That depends. RAM chips are usually organized so that each chip contributes one of the bits of an eight-bit word. That means that eight chips make up a memory module. 4Kx1 chips are now readily available and they are packing more circuits into a single chip all the time.
Willy:	With so many circuits how can I be sure to read or write to or from a specific location?
Computer:	Well, for example, for a 1Kx1 chip you need 10 address lines $(2^{10} = 1024 = 1K)$ to point to a unique location on the chip. Each of the eight chips in the module made up of eight 1Kx1 chips are presented with the same address.
Willy:	But you said there were 16 address lines. What about the other six?
Computer:	They are used to constrict a chip-select signal. You remember we talked about tri-state devices. The trick is not to enable a chip (leave it in the high impedance state) unless it is being addressed.
Willy:	I'm not sure I know what you mean by constricting a chip select signal. Would you tell me a little more about it?
Computer:	Sure. All you need to do is construct some simple digital logic so that the output of your logic is not true unless the highest

	six address lines are correct. You can also use some special chips like decoders or comparators to do the same thing. I guess I should warn you that some memory chips have more than one chip-select pin. This complicates things a little, but the idea is still the same.
Willy:	Anything else I should know about RAM's?
Computer:	Well, timing is quite important before you can decide whether a given memory chip will work for any given microcomputer. The memory has to be fast enough to allow the CPU to access it. If it is not, there will be a terrible crash of data trying to get in and out. In other words, the memory won't know whether it's coming or going.
Willy:	Why don't designers just use the fastest memory chips possible?
Computer:	Cost! It gets pretty expensive using fast RAM. If the designer of a memory board knows ahead of time that the memory chips are too slow for the CPU, he can arrange to tell the CPU to insert special wait states into the cycle which gives the memory chips additional time to present valid data.
Willy:	OK, now I think I understand a little about read-write memory or RAM's. But a question occurs to me. If dynamic memory is harder to use than static, why do people even use them?
Computer:	It's true that dynamic memory has some complications, but they are attractive to a designer because they are always cheaper, can be produced with a higher density of bits for a given area, and consume less power than static memory.
Willy:	Now, what about these ROM's and PROM's you threw about before?
Computer:	All of those memory chips are read-only memory chips. That is, when you use them you can only read out permanently stored data and cannot write data into a memory location.
Willy:	I got you! If you can't write data into them how do you put the data on the chip that you said you could read out?
Computer:	That's done ahead of time with a special programming technique that involves writing data into the chip with a high voltage that is applied many times. Voltages run around 28 volts and a high voltage pulse may have to be applied from 100 to 1000 times.

74

Willy:	I guess with voltages that high it means the data is really there forever. Am I correct?
Computer:	Yes and no. A ROM is programmed by the manufacturer from a custom mask. This involves a high initial cost like $10,000, so you'd better need a lot of identical ROM's to make it worthwhile. A PROM, that stands for **Programmable *R*ead *O*nly *M*emory,** can be programmed in the field by special PROM programmers starting from a standard blank chip, which means they cost a lot less. In the case of the PROM, the programming involves melting a fusible link just like a fuse for a zero and leaving the connection for a one. The EPROM, which stands for **Erasable *P*rogrammable *R*ead *O*nly *M*emory,** can also be programmed in the field, but uses a different process. The high voltage causes a semi-permanent bond to impress the information on the chip. However, because of the special behavior of the material, if the chip is exposed to a large dose of short wavelength ultraviolet light, things are restored to the original unprogrammed state and new information can be programmed. New developments are going on which are producing electrically erasable ROM's where you can write or erase one bit at a time. Hobby microcomputers mostly use the UV erasable chips.
Willy:	Are read-only memories organized like RAM's with each chip furnishing only one bit of the eight-bit byte?
Computer:	No. usually read-only memories are organized like 1Kx8 or even 2Kx8 with a single chip furnishing all of the eight data bits from a given addressable location.
Willy:	Are you hiding anything from me? Have you told me about all the various kinds of memory I might run into?
Computer:	Not quite. There are some advanced types that are still under development or not used in hobby microcomputers. They have esoteric names like bubble memory, charge-coupled devices, cache memory, etc., but again I think we better leave those for another book.
Willy:	I've got a nagging question bothering me. These memory chips are complicated. How do we know that they are working correctly? Do they ever give you wrong information? From what we talked about before in Software, I can see that even one bit in error could cause a disaster in a program
Computer:	You are absolutely correct. Even though they are generally

tested thoroughly during production, some bad chips slip through and some failures can occur long after they have been installed in your machine. It is good practice to run programs called memory testers to check the chip. They usually write a series of varying patterns of zero's and one's into each location and then check by reading the same location if the proper word is stored there. Even then peculiar things happen and writing a word into one location can cause another location to drop a bit. Those errors are hard to find and really exhaustive memory testing can take enormous amounts of machine time to run. Those kinds of errors show up usually when a program that has been running fine suddenly starts to get clobbered.

Willy: That's great. I wouldn't claim to be an expert on memory yet, but I think I understand the basics. But, I realize that a microcomputer has to do things like get characters from a terminal, write them on a CRT, and print results. How are these things implemented in hardware?

I/O AND YOU

Computer: You've certainly got a logical mind. Now that we've talked about the CPU and memory, the next step is to talk about how the microcomputer talks and listens to the outside world. What we are talking about now is input and output, which again in computereze is called I/O.

Willy: Now I bet you're going to tell me that there are different kinds of I/O just to complicate life for me. Am I right?

Computer: On the money! We're going to have to talk about parallel and serial I/O for starters.

Willy: I remember the word parallel from high school geometry. What does it mean in a computer I/O?

Computer: Parallel means that all eight bits of a word you wish to input or output from the microcomputer are put on eight individual signal lines, and you transmit the whole byte simultaneously. Usually you only use parallel I/O for transmitting data a short distance. If you were sending data over a telephone line, you'd like to find another scheme or else you would be paying toll charges for each of the eight data lines.

Willy: Is there only one set of eight lines for parallel I/O in a microcomputer?

Computer:	Oh, no. You can have many more. We talk about I/O ports. One way to address an I/O port is to use port addressing. This takes up only eight address lines, which means, if you remember your binary arithmetic, there are $2^8 = 256$ different input ports and 256 output ports available. By the way, input always means *to* the CPU, while output means *from* the CPU to the outside world. On the other hand, memory-mapped addressing looks at an I/O port just as if it were a memory address. In this case you could have literally thousands of I/O ports.
Willy:	That seems a little silly to me. Why would you need more than 256 I/O ports?
Computer:	Numbers are not the real reason. If you remember from programming, there are only two instructions for an I/O port: IN and OUT. With memory-mapped I/O, any instruction that references memory is OK.
Willy:	That's pretty clear. But I think I see a problem. If I have a number of I/O ports, what happens if they all try to talk to me at once.
Computer:	First of all, remember what we said about tri-state devices and chip-selects. This will let us make sure that only the device selected from the address buss can take data or put data on the data buss.
Willy:	I'm still worried about how I'll know which device I'm talking to.
Computer:	Well, in addition to eight signal lines for data we also have control lines to indicate which device needs service from the CPU. This brings up what we call "handshaking." Imagine that when a device needs service it sends out a "1" on a control line which is stored in, say, a flip-flop. If I continually look at these service-request flip-flops, I will know which device I've got to deal with.
Willy:	I need more help. What do you mean with this handshaking routine?
Computer:	Suppose I'm the CPU and I want to send a word to you through an I/O port. Call me the "talker" and we'll call you the "listener." We will deal with two signals on two control lines, one called data available (DAV) and one called data accepted (DAC). Look at the picture I've drawn so you can follow me: Now it goes like this. 1) I know my DAV line is 0. I look and see your DAC line is also 0. Great! I send the word to the

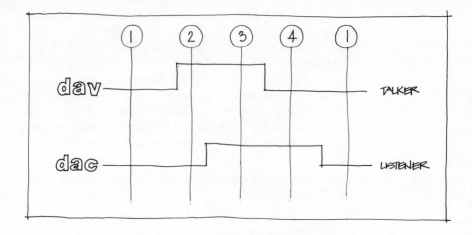

I/O port, where it is held in a latch. (If you don't know what a latch is don't worry. It's just an IC chip that holds eight bits of data and doesn't change until new data is sent to it.) 2) To let you know a byte is ready for you to read, I set DAV to a 1. 3) Now you get in the act. You read the data and let me know by setting DAC to a 1. 4) My turn. I want you to know that I saw you accept the data, so I pull down DAV, that is, put a 0 on it. This makes sure that you won't read the byte more than one time. 1) Again — You finish up by pulling down DAC (0). Our little transaction is over and we are both back where we started and can use the whole routine over again to send another byte of data if necessary. There's no reason why we couldn't reverse roles and you would be the talker and I the listener.

Willy: I think I've got it. Both of us have to be pretty smart to do all this. Is there some other way?

Computer: Sure. The way I've described it there would have to be a program in the microcomputer and some logic designed for the device. It turns out it is relatively simple to hardwire the whole procedure. For example, suppose you were a keyboard and you wanted to send me a character. The instant you hit the key, a flip-flop would be set to a 1 so I know you put out a character. The instant the CPU reads the character, a little circuitry would reset the flip-flop (3). The CPU runs so much faster than your fingers that there's no danger that you can type faster than I can read. Also, since I only read a character when the flip-flop is a 1, and the act of reading the byte of data resets the flip-flop, there's no danger of

	my making and reading the same character many times while you're getting ready to send a new one.
Willy:	Very clever. How do I know you are going to notice my setting the flip-flop when I hit that key?
Computer:	This method is called "polling." By that I mean that the CPU gives one or more I/O ports its undivided attention. It just sits in a program loop reading those flip-flops, waiting for a 1. As soon as a device requests service it gets it just as I just described. I've got a secret, though. This polling technique completely ties up the CPU. The only job you can assign it is to look at those flip-flops.
Willy:	That doesn't seem right. Here I buy this hot-shot computer and don't demand much from him. Can't you figure out some other way to do it?
Computer:	I have a feeling you know the answer to that question is yes. We use a technique called "interrupts." Here's how it works. The CPU is doing some useful task. When a device needs the CPU for service, it sends a signal along the control buss to a special interrupt pin on the CPU chip. The CPU notices this and as soon as it finishes the current instruction, it sends a signal that acknowledges the interrupt request. At this point the device that interrupted has the responsibility to put a byte of data on the data buss that tells the CPU where to go in memory to find a program that will service the device (for instance, a program to read a character from a keyboard like we just talked about). When the CPU finishes this service routine it goes back to where it was before being interrupted until it is again interrupted. I think that you see how we can keep the CPU busy and only stop its work when an I/O device needs attention.
Willy:	That sounds complicated, or am I just dumb?
Computer:	No, it is complicated and I've given you a very simple view of interrupts. There are lots of things I haven't told you. The CPU needs a way to decide what to do when more than one device interrupts at the same time, and there are times when the CPU is doing something which would get fouled up by an interrupt. That's taken care of by giving the CPU the ability to ignore interrupt. If you're a device requesting an interrupt at such a time, you're going to have to wait a while.
Willy:	Well, now I know everything about parallel I/O. Right?
Computer:	You know better than that. I could talk for an awful long

time about special IC chips that have three I/O ports and have all the handshaking and interrupt capability hard-wired. What's more, these chips can operate in many different modes that are under the control of software (a program that gives the chip its marching orders as to how to operate). There are also other IC's that are just as smart and take care of as many as eight devices that may want to request interrupts and sorts out who gets top priority in case of more than one interruption at the same time.

Willy: Listen, please don't put me down. I'm learning. I'm even smart enough to remember you said something about serial I/O some time ago. What's that?

Computer: Serial I/O uses only a single signal line to transmit and receive data.

Willy: I got you! How do you send an eight-bit word then?

Computer: One bit at a time! We'll agree ahead of time that I'll send bit O first so you know the order.

Willy: Does a teletype send and receive serially?

Computer: Yes.

Willy: They are awfully slow. How can they keep up with a CPU that goes like lightning?

Computer: First of all we will use handshaking so that data is only sent or received when both parties are ready. We also need to arrange it so that the bits are sent at a prearranged rate. We call bits per second "baud rate."

Willy: I'm not clear about all that. What did you really say?

Computer: First of all, I may want to send you characters asynchronously. That's a fancy word that means I may send ten characters and then wait a while and send a few more some time later. I think you can see that the sender is going to have to let the receiver know when a character begins and ends, otherwise if the sender stops transmitting, the receiver might think he is sending lots of zero's. We call this framing. At the beginning of a character we transmit a start bit and after the bits of the word are sent we transmit one or more stop bits indicating the word is over. The receiver now just waits until he gets a new start bit before he decodes the signal lines as data. Since the baud rate (bits/second) determines how long a one or a zero will be sent out before the next bit is sent, that requires what we call clocks at both ends that are running at the same rate to keep the timing problems in hand. Teletypes

	run at 110 baud, yet on the high-speed end we may send data to a CRT terminal at up to 9600 baud.
Willy:	I got it. You use start and stop bits so everyone knows where a transmitted word begins and ends, and clocks for timing. Right?
Computer:	Almost. Remember we are talking about asynchronous serial data transmission. There is another kind called synchronous serial transmission. Here the message starts with a special word to alert the receiver, and from then on data is transmitted continuously with no stopping. This is used mostly for high-speed data transmission, and gets pretty complicated, so let's drop it at that.
Willy:	Ok with me. I've got my hands full already. Are the programs you need to write for serial transmission complicated?
Computer:	They can be. Luckily most of the work can be done in hardware with special IC chips. We have chips called UART's, which stands for **U**niversal **A**synchronous **R**eceive and **T**ransmit. The chip automatically will receive an eight-bit parallel data word and then arrange to put out serially the start bit, then the individual data bits, and then the stop bits. But it does more. The chip provides the signals we talked about for handshaking or interrupts and even does more by checking for errors in transmission or errors caused by sending a new word before the old one was read, etc.
Willy:	My head is tired. Are you finished with I/O?
Computer:	One thing more occurred to me. That's the nature of the signal transmitted over our line. If you recall we talked for the microcomputer of voltages of 0 to 5 volts for a zero or a one. In serial transmission, the industry has adopted a different standard called EIA-RS232C. It talks about a lot of electrical specifications so that everyone does things the same way. They use strange voltage surges like -36v to +36v with specified bands of negative and positive voltages to represent zero's and one's. Some serial transmission schemes don't even use voltages to represent zero's and one's. Instead of voltages, a closed electrical loop is wired and the presence of an electrical current represents a one and no current represents a zero. It's called a 20MA current loop. I didn't mean to make an electrical engineer out of you, but don't worry. There are some very simple electronic circuits and even some inexpensive IC chips that convert back and forth from the computer's 0 to 5 volts to the other system.

Willy:	Boy!! These last few minutes have been action-packed as far as learning something new.
Computer:	If you give me a minute, I'll take an hour.
Willy:	You could probably take four hours.
Computer:	If you knew as much about yourself as I do about myself, you could talk for hours, too!
Willy:	Well, there's no ego lost in your family.
Computer:	What's an ego?
Willy:	Oh! Forget it.
Computer:	Let's not; I would really like to know.
Willy:	Actually I don't have the time. Besides we have probably lost half the people reading this book because we have gotten too technical.
Computer:	I really can't understand; all it takes is a logical mind to be able to follow along.
Willy:	You don't have any feelings about people! There are different types you know, and they don't all learn the same way!
Computer:	Who says I don't have feelings — my programmer says I do. He talks to me all the time.
Willy:	Ya! But he's not of this world, either.
Computer:	1000111100111110101001001111100100010001011001100 1001100
Willy:	Now! Now! This is supposed to be a family book. If we printed that out it wouldn't look very good for you.
Computer:	I'm sorry!
Willy:	Let's get back to it then. Since we have covered the CPU, busses, RAM, and I/O, what's left?
Computer:	Two things: mass storage and peripherals.
Willy:	Oh, I know what mass storage is. It's what you use to store programs and data on the outside of you.
Computer:	You're absolutely right. Boy! You catch on very quickly.
Willy:	Thank you!
Computer:	Let's talk about audio cassette first. This method was introduced into home computing because of its ease of usage and the inexpensive circuits that it needs. Also an average stand-

ard home cassette recorder can be used.

Willy:	You mean that my tape recorder is actually a piece of computer equipment?
Computer:	Well, in a way. What some engineers have come up with is a way of developing tones that can be read as zero's and one's. The way it works is the interface that's plugged into my buss structure has a group of circuits that will take an 8-bit word, that's coming off the data buss, and convert it to a frequency shifting tone. Because the byte comes in in a parallel fashion, the interface first converts it to a serial bit stream, then checks and sees if it is a zero or a one, and converts it to a tone. This then is sent out over a normal mike cable to the input on the cassette deck itself.
Willy:	Ah, hah!
Computer:	Wake up, Willy, you're dozing off.
Willy:	I'm tired!
Computer:	What's tired mean?
Willy:	Forget it.
Computer:	Anyway, just the reverse happens when we take data or programs from the recorder and put them into memory. This serial data that is transferred on and off the cassette tape is done at a fairly fast speed. When we were discussing I/O earlier I talked about baud rate. Well, the transfer rate, or baud rate, for a normal audio cassette is about 1600 bits per second. This converts to about 200 bytes per second. Are you following?
Willy:	Yes!
Computer:	These shifting frequency tones are generated at 1200 cycles and 2400 cycles per second.
	Even though audio cassette units are widely used, it still isn't the best way to store data. Stretching tape, dirty read and record heads, and wow and flutter in the recorder itself add to bad data transfer. We get better and faster results with a floppy disk.
Willy:	Boy, am I getting tired!
Computer:	Just a few more minutes. Floppy disks look like a 45 RPM record that's encased in a paper jacket. This disk spins at a speed of 360 RPM and the data transfer is much faster; 40,000 bits per second is the transfer rate.

Willy:	Wow!
Computer:	The floppy disk read/write head only comes in contact with the diskette itself during a read or write function.
Willy:	You mean it's lifting off from the diskette all the time?
Computer:	That's right!
Willy:	Ya know, I think we have probably confused our readers enough already. Can we stop now?
Computer:	I have just one more thing.
Willy:	What's that?
Computer:	I would like to talk about what the process is when a home computer user types on a keyboard and it appears on my CRT screen.
Willy:	OK. But that's it. I've got to go before the tape recorder runs out.
Computer:	Back when I was talking about I/O, we discussed parallel and serial, remember?
Willy:	Oh, yeah! Parallel is sending all eight bits of the byte at one time and serial is one bit at a time, am I right?
Computer:	Your memory banks astonish me.
Willy:	Thanks.
Computer:	Anyway, the sending device or terminal we have been talking about uses a serial type of I/O. When a human types a key on the keyboard, the terminal yields a string of bit pulses along a cable. This transmits data from the terminal, and it goes into the receive data line in the serial I/O board. The serial I/O board then converts this serial bit stream to an eight-bit byte, and sends it to the controller, my brain.
Willy:	Wait a minute. Why doesn't the eight bits go right into the CPU?
Computer:	Because the CPU needs to review all eight bits at once. Let me push on. When the controller receives the byte, it then echoes the byte back to the I/O board to be sent out. When the serial I/O gets the byte back, it changes it back from all eight bits to a serial stream, and sends the byte back to the terminal. The I/O board at this point is transmitting data and the terminal is receiving data. Then the character is displayed on my CRT screen.
Willy:	Boy! That sure is a lot of running around. It must take a long time to go back and forth like that.

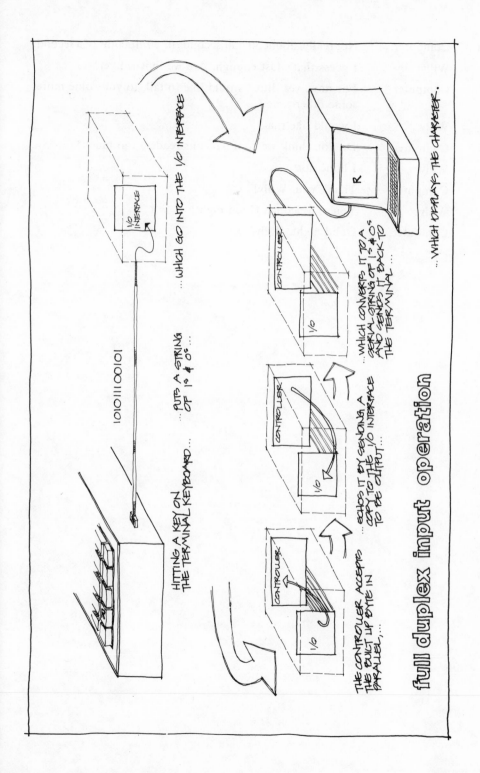

1010111100101

HITTING A KEY ON
THE TERMINAL KEYBOARD...

...PUTS A STRING
OF 1s & 0s...

...WHICH GO INTO THE I/O INTERFACE

I/O
INTERFACE

CONTROLLER

I/O

CONTROLLER

I/O

CONTROLLER

I/O

R

THE CONTROLLER ACCEPTS
THE BUILT UP BYTE IN
PARALLEL,...

...ECHOS IT BY SENDING A
COPY TO THE I/O INTERFACE
TO BE OUTPUT...

...WHICH CONVERTS IT TO A
SERIAL STRING OF 1s & 0s
AND SENDS IT BACK TO
THE TERMINAL...

...WHICH DISPLAYS THE CHARACTER.

full duplex input operation

85

Computer:	Not really, about 50 milliseconds or 50/1000ths of a second.
Willy:	I guess that's fast enough. Are we finished yet?
Computer:	For now, yes. But I would like to talk to you some more, some other time.
Willy:	I would like that.
Computer:	Do you think we confused our readers too much?
Willy:	I hope not!
Computer:	Thank you, Willy!
Willy:	You're welcome. Good night!
Computer:	Good night, Willy.

VII.

WHAT CAN I DO WITH IT?

The question most often asked of me is "What can you do with a personal computer?" The possibilities are endless, so I usually answer "Anything that you need a tablet of paper, a pencil, and a hand-held calculator for, you can do faster, more reliably, and more accurately with a personal computer." The following list covers just a few such uses. Let your imagination go and you will be able to come up with many more possibilities!

Recordkeeping

Inventory management

Routine correspondence and form letters

Filling out forms

Calculations of all kinds

Receiving and placing phone calls

MATCHING any information with any other information.

Polls and surveys

Indexing

Cataloging

Solving problems

Printing out results

Engineering design aid

Maintaining *LISTS,* especially:

  MAILING LISTS

  SHOPPING LISTS

  ITEMIZATIONS

  STOCKLISTS

  PACKING LISTS

Sales analysis

Travel and route planning

Scheduling

Ticketing

Distribution

Scientific calculations

Education

Accounting and billing

Invoicing

Sorting

Receipts

Taxes

Addressing

Budgets

Forecasting

Reducing the physical *SIZE of FILES* (customer files, correspondence, product files, etc.) — *No more file cabinets!!!*

Playing games

Cashflow

Maintaining "tickle-files" (calendar-reminder systems)

Filling out checks

Playing the stock market

FILING

Remembering all transactions

Making and keeping card catalogs

"Simulating" results of one action versus others, so you can compare their outcomes

Editing

The majority of people who have looked at the personal computer marketplace today have seen only the game playing side of it. They probably think computers are cousins to the video games now on the market. Though you can use a personal computer to play video games, it is not fair to limit personal computers to game playing. Don't get me wrong, video games are a great pastime and a different application for the home TV, but a personal computer can do so much more. In this chapter I will touch on just a few of the possible home, hobby, school, and business applications possible with a personal computer.

GAMES COMPUTERS PLAY

The games that are now being run on computers are more "simulations" than anything else. What I mean by "simulation" can be demonstrated by one of the most popular games people are running on their home computers, *Star*

Trek. *Star Trek* players, as part of the game, have to locate and destroy a number of Klingon war ships before running out of moves or fuel.

The game is laid out on a grid of squares, usually 10 x 10, called quadrants. Within each quadrant are 10 x 10 grids, called sectors. As the captain of the Starship *Enterprise,* you have the fortunate duty of destroying all Klingon war ships within a certain number of moves. The Klingon war ships are located randomly in any sector of any quadrant.

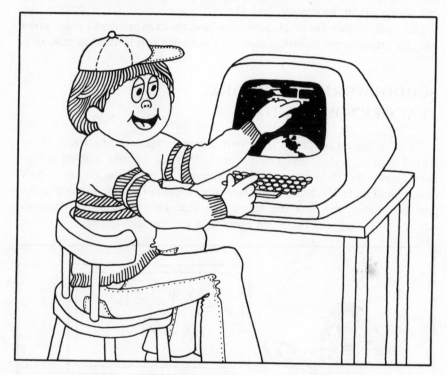

At your disposal you have short and long-range sensors, probes, star bases on which you can refuel and redeposit weapons, warp engines to move you around, and torpedoes and phasers to shoot down the enemy. It all sounds very complicated, but if you ever play, you will keep coming back to try new strategies.

During the course of play, unconsciously you are falling back on the basics of math you have learned in school. Angles and vectors, for example, are used to move from one sector to another, or in directing the torpedoes toward their Klingon targets. Basic physics come into play when weapons or warp engines are used. As you fire or move your ship around, power is consumed rapidly and you are forced to calculate where your nearest star base is so you can refuel.

If battling with the Klingon empire is not your cup of tea, you can try your luck with any number of casino games. Blackjack, poker, dice and roulette programs are available now for your computer. Just think of being able to play blackjack against the house, your computer, with a million dollars in your pocket. You can be just like the high rollers we have seen and heard about, and not really lose a dime.

For the more serious-minded there is always chess, backgammon, checkers, and raja. If any of the existing games are not appealing to you, you can always create your own.

Thus, not only do personal computers have the excitement of a video game but you are required to utilize some of the basics you learned in school.

SCHOOLWORK, HOMEWORK, TEACHER'S WORK, TOO

All of us are aware of the large part television plays in education. Many school systems today have closed-circuit TV's for lectures and classroom demonstrations. Public broadcasting stations all over the country show educational material throughout the day and night. The video screen of the personal computer turns the magic box that kids are glued to into an educational machine. There are numerous programs available today that

have been developed to use a game simulation and work in a math drill at the same time.

If you are a teacher you could use a personal computer as a *TUTORIAL AID* and to do *INSTANT GRADING,* for example. Perhaps, above all, you can use it to *TEACH PROGRAMMING.* And the students will have to write programs to DO something, so they start coming up with interesting applications. (Programming boosts mathematical ability; it's not the other way around, as often supposed.) The kids find themselves exposed to possibilities like all these we're taking about. They catch on quick what to do with them!

Perhaps one of the most important things kids can discover is how to earn a living in a way that feels creative to them. And again we see the personal computers playing a *big* part in exactly this discovery!

Meanwhile, the personal computer can help with *HOMEWORK.* And it can feature in all sorts of projects and reports, ones that get writeups in local papers. This often happens with student computer projects, because they tend to be so original. Also, one student can do the work of many this way. And many scientific projects become possible with a computer that were impossible before.

DON'T BOUNCE THAT CHECK

Your personal computer can serve a very useful purpose in helping you with your own personal finances. There are checkbook balancing programs available that are much like a general ledger system for a small business. They give you a charge of accounts or slots for storing check information. For instance, you can set up categories such as "rent" or "mortgage," "food," "insurance," "clothing," "utilities," "entertainment." Each time you write a check you enter the information into one of these categories. At the end of the year all of the necessary information would be stored in these categories for use in your income tax. At tax time you can use a tax program to compute your tax return for the year.

Budget programs exist that allow you to forecast your expenses for an entire year and enable you to plan investments for the future.

LIST TO YOUR HEART'S CONTENT

Computers are fantastic at working with lists. The nice thing is that you can change anything in the list — even one letter, "B," for example — without affecting the rest. It's like a stored-away blackboard. As items become obsolete — the way they're always doing in a shopping list, say — you just tell your computer to "drop" them from the list. Your computer does the rest: *YOU DON'T HAVE TO KEEP WRITING THE LIST OVER AGAIN.*

THIS GOES FOR ANY COLLECTION OF INFORMATION IN YOUR COMPUTER — YOU DON'T HAVE TO REDO THE WHOLE THING OVER JUST TO CHANGE ONE PART.

This makes your computer a powerful tool for such things as *TEXT EDITING.* You can work a whole manuscript over without having to erase or "fix" anything, physically. The savings in time alone are immense — in writing, editing, and composition! But imagine *USING NO PAPER* until you've got the *final version!* I will discuss computer lists and text editing again later in this chapter.

HOBBYIST HELP GALORE

We all have hobbies at one time or another. You would probably be surprised at what a personal computer could do to assist you in whatever that hobby is.

If you are any kind of a collector, for instance, your computer can categorize your collection and index it for you. You can keep pertinent information such as transaction dates, model numbers, descriptions, and the up-to-date value of your inventory. It can also help you select the piece to go after next, when looking to add to your collection.

If you are a model builder or a craftsman, your computer can keep records on inventories for your building needs. Charts, graphs, diagrams, and blueprints can be filed and indexed for you. With the graphics capabilities of some computers, you would be able to design and layout your next project.

You can see from these few samples of home computer applications that the computer works marvelously in two ways for you: *Improvement and Expansion.* Improvement: your computer will do for you what you're already doing, in a fraction of the time. Expansion: you do things with it you could never have done before.

IMPROVEMENT — BUSINESS COMPUTING

If you're in mail-order, own a small business, or work in an office profession, a microcomputer is for you! It can keep your **mailing lists** and print **address labels** at a rate of four per second, all accurate and up-to-date. It can store all your records on products, sales, customers, and ad results. It will compare or change any part of these you'd like, without touching the rest. In other words, it gives you *SALES ANALYSIS* and *MARKET PROFILES* which only "multimillionaires" have had until now!

Your computer *keeps inventories.*

It does *accounting* and *billing* of all types.

It does *order entry* (live).

It can hold and index your *"own private library"* of whatever information interests you.

For example, it can help in health care by keeping track of each patient's medical history and alerting you to patterns you might have missed. Or give you a quick way to look up the newest therapies by *what* they *remedy* — you type in the condition and your computer gives you back a list of indicated drugs or treatment.

If you are a pharmacist, you may presently be keeping "card files" of each customer's contraindications and other medication history. With a computer, you'd no longer have to look each of these up for each prescription! You'd just type in the customer's name and Rx, and up would come the pertinent information on a little TV screen, just like at the airlines. You could also tell your computer to remember a list of "potentiating" drug combinations and warn you if it detects one in a customer's combination. *YOU DON'T HAVE TO THINK IT OUT OR LOOK IT UP EACH TIME, ANY MORE.*

Your computer can run *FLEXIBLE FORM LETTERS* for you! You tell it to change this word or that, add or delete a paragraph, date a letter next Monday, and address it to, say, all the people in your "Best Prospects" file. Out will come a stack of letters, individualized and ready to mail! Because of the "add-on" equipment which adapts computers for particular jobs we arrive at your computer's greatest promise: expansion.

EXPANSION — COMPUTER BUSINESSES

You're about to see what *new types of business* are possible with a computer running in your home! These are all high-profit, high-service businesses — yet they take little space or time. Best of all, they're *very low in stress!* Let's face it, one of the chief causes of *STRESS* seems to be *EMPLOYMENT.* It's hard on both *worker* and *boss.* So why be *either?* Get a computer.

Here are some new businesses one person alone can set up with a computer. The first are all based on one thing computers do very well: information-matching! Basically this gives you a *CLASSIFIED AD SERVICE,* either general or very special (like clothing only). And it can be "live," available right over the phone. So, *LIVE CLASSIFIED ADS* are a very *LIVE BUSINESS OPPORTUNITY!* It works like this: people call to say they want this or have that, and you tell them who has or wants it. You do this by signalling your computer what's offered or wanted. In a few seconds it gives you a *list* of people who have or want that thing! You read that to your caller.

Your computer will display any desired details you've given it in the past, as part of the list. The point is, *YOU* don't have to *REMEMBER* it all anymore. So your "data bank" can be much larger than you could ever handle mentally, and you're able to give far broader service. At the same time you're freed up for creative work!

Moreover, some phone companies are learning to cooperate by "On-Call Billing" of calls to your service number. The caller is simply charged a higher rate for calling that number. These charges are then forwarded or credited by the phone company directly to you. In other words, as a business *you get paid when you're called.*

Where On-Call Billing isn't available yet, you can tie-in your fee with transactions, like the New York 'Buylines' do. This is more work, but that's what your computer does anyhow.

Some new satellites are making phone lines unnecessary, and getting clearer transmission to boot. Your "phone system" can become very powerful, with help like this. By "being in" with a system ahead of time, you can make the most of it.

NEW BUSINESSES

Real Estate — With up-to-the-minute listings over a wide area.

Dating Service — Getting people together. With speedy, detailed descriptions that *you* don't have to look up! (Your computer will spot the most "ideal matches.")

Apartment and Building Rental Service — Where subscribers can find *places for rent,* or list places they have. There's a need for this kind of service, since real estate agencies are more interested in sales. If you have an agency, however, a computer lets you *expand painlessly* into rentals. With a computer you can make your service "long distance," too, using classifieds from other cities.

Swapping Service — You put people who need and have things they want to trade in touch with each other. Instead of money, they give you "due bills" which you charge 10% each on. These act as "certificates" for exchanging the goods or service. For example, you know a dentist who wants a used car and a car dealer who wants his house painted. Your *COMPUTER* completes the circle; it displays the name of a painter who needs dental work! You have due-bills from each already, and just put the people in touch. And you get paid with each due bill, so it doesn't matter to you whether they go ahead with the swap or not.

Equipment Rental Service — Here your computer merely keeps tabs on who has equipment they are willing to rent and who wants to rent some.

Again, *YOU DON'T HAVE TO STOCK ANYTHING.* Furniture, housegoods, and even cars can be rented.

Shopper's "Where to Find It" Service — This is like a detailed "Department Store Directory" available by phone. Your computer keeps track of what stores carry which items, and prices too if you wish! You can also notify of specials and sales.

Instant Babysitting — You run a "register" of baby sitters who are available on short notice. This can be used for many other types of jobs and services, too, of course.

"Phone Rummage" Sales — Like a rural version of the "What's For Sale" service. The big items can even be *catalogued* into your system, so callers can ask, say, for a piano and you'll know where there is one for sale. Such a system can be applied to flea markets, too.

Clothing Clearinghouse — This answers an acute need. Everybody — especially females and children — had a predicament until now: they need different nice things to wear, and they have good clothes they don't want. Yet they're unable to sell or find a used *thing!* (If you'd seen how little a store offers you for a perfectly good gown that's been worn only once, you'd know why!). This is a natural for a computer. You just keep pumping it full of clothing descriptions and clients' names and phone numbers, and your computer will find every match there is, even down to desired color and size! After you've brought two parties together they can work out any terms they wish about the clothing. You get paid by the phone company, or by clients for the numbers you give them. You *DON'T HAVE TO KEEP ANY CLOTHING ON HAND.* You need no extra space and no merchandise to conduct this business.

Now for some businesses that are not of the "information matching" type. Notice that these still take almost no space to operate.

Service Bureau — Doing small business work for other people or firms. Accounting, billing, payroll, mailings, correspondence, taxes, and inventory are top candidates. You can do for *others* anything we've named so far.

Answering Service — Fully automated. We think that with a little ingenuity you could run a whole answering service using nothing but a phone and your computer. Go off to the Health Club while your computer routes messages all day!

Calling Service — Your computer, properly rigged, can do much of your routine phone calling for you. You can even tell it to call someone from across the room! (And will remember the number — all you have to know is the name.) Some people will use a computer to place automatic "buy-sell" orders on the stock market or commodities. You could be earning in two places at once! You'd be at your job or business, while your computer is playing the stocks for you!

Horoscopes — Your computer can cast horoscopes, and then print them out for you to use. It's able to mix "individual" information such as birthdate and place, with the "mass" information ahead of time.) It can then print out horoscopes in as many copies as you wish, with the people's names and addresses on them for mailing. Such horoscope services are now advertised nationally.

Tarot Readings — This is the same idea as horoscopes, only the "general" information you give your computer beforehand is from books on the Tarot instead of astrology. Your computer could "draw" the cards for you! Tarot readings are becoming popular and more novel to the public than horoscopes.

Writing Service — Your computer is the best assistant editor anyone ever had. How it saves *TIME!* And *PAPER.*

Classified Bulletin — Publish it monthly or bi-weekly. It has nothing but classified ads of all kinds. The ads are run *FREE* and people pay you when there's a sale. This sounds risky, but for many reasons, *it works.* A classified bulletin is a much better deal for people than the newspaper — all you need is adequate coverage. People's ads run longer, run *free,* and cover better geographical area. You could be running a "live" classified service and a printed version, at the same time. Each serves as publicity for the other. You could also support your classified bulletin with paid ads from local businesses.

Other new businesses possible with your computer:

Local Events Calendar

Reservations Service

Opinion Polls and Surveys

Lotteries and other Fortune Games

Betting Systems — winning at
  horses, blackjack, etc. It can
  be done, in fact it *IS.* And
  there are some books on it.

Golf Handicapping

News Service

Ticketron

Problem Solving for Others

Special Interest Clubs

Selling time on your computer. You
  charge other people for using it.

Your own Publication — magazine
  classified, or newsletter, editing
  with the computer.

HOW A COMPUTER CAN HELP YOU IN YOUR HOME

With all of these uses, you must already have some ideas about what one of these "mighty midgets" can do in your home! First you can have everything controlled automatically, whether you're there or not.

Your home computer can literally become your "private secretary." You'll feel like the President, as it keeps track of notes, dates, reminders, appointments . . . It will alert you at the right time, give you a message that "school's letting out early today," that "So-and-So's coming to visit," that "you have an appointment downtown at 2:00." It will keep lists, balance your checkbook, be a library, manage your finances, and answer the door. *YOUR MIND GETS UNBURDENED* — a computer's really useful for that! It may even **prevent wrinkles,** if those come from feeling harassed.

Right now, you'll "tell" your computer what you want by typing messages on its keyboard. Don't worry how it "understands" them. It does. Just type your instructions, and it will do the rest.

You'll even be able to *SPEAK* your commands to it, and it will carry them out! For example, there's an alarm clock on the market **right now** that stops ringing if you yell at it. (If you just groan or talk, it rings less.) And it recognizes **your** voice — no one else's!

Any electrical device can be set up to do this. We've always liked the idea of *lights* that keep themselves on **only when someone's around.** (You wouldn't have to talk to them, they'd know you were there by your body temperature.)

As each of these technical devices comes onto the market, you'll be ready. You can just *ADD* them to your system.

Your computer can also help with **home protection.** It's hard to beat a trained attack dog, of course. But he can't call the Fire Department if he smells smoke, or signal your "beeper" when the baby wakes up. And you don't have to **walk** your computer. For burglar protection, as a matter of fact, a little machine is planned that attaches to your front door. When activated, if anyone starts tampering with your door while you're away, it will *sound* like a ferocious dog roaring and hitting the door. Your computer can do even better, especially if you have a Hi-Fi set.

It could even be wired to water plants or feed fish.

At home as in business, your computer's *YOUR PARTNER IN JUDGMENT!!* And it helps with all kinds of planning. You can do budgets, schedules, calendars, party management, and inventory, and keep your own "mailing lists" and phone directory. You can do super MENU-PLANNING with a computer, too. It tells you what's in the refrigerator, what you're out of, what needs using up, and what you'll need to buy for a certain recipe. Or it tells you what recipes you can do with what's on hand. Frankly, all this would be a big order for your little computer at present. But it's coming. (Also, the longer you spend with your system, the more versatile it gets.)

Remember how easily your computer handles *LISTS*. Well, you can add or delete items all week, and review it anytime you want. Only those items you changed would be different. And the rest of the time your lists are tucked away safe and *CLUTTER FREE!*

Now more on *TEXT EDITING,* because it's so well suited to work at (The sources of editing work to do at home are so varied that we won't go into them here. The most common is *TYPING,* of course.)

You type your material into the computer, which "stores" it in its memory. Then you call up the material section by section, and work it over. *YOU USE NO PAPER.* You don't have to erase, or "fix," or buy correction fluid. You won't have to make carbons. Any change you call for is made instantaneously. After the work is *EXACTLY THE WAY YOU WANT IT,* you press the "PRINT" button. Then your system spits out finished pages. The newest systems do this *a complete page at a time,* and silently like a Xerox.

INDEXING

We don't know if you're into indexing or not. If you have a lot of ideas or keep a diary or want to save clippings and the like, though, *INDEXING* is for you. It creates a compact filing system, ready to go — and your computer's the one to do it! It will keep track of all the headings, key words, page or issue numbers, and the alphabetization of everything. Here's how it works, basic-ally: Say you have a clipping or an idea you want to "index," perhaps about a car that runs on sunpower. You tell your computer the key words for the idea or article — like "FUELLESS CAR" — and then tell your computer where you've put the writeup on it, "file of October '77, Item Number 4."

When you want to look up the article again, you just tell your computer the *KEY WORDS* — type in "FUELLESS CAR" — and your computer will tell you exactly where to look for the writeup! (You might have collected several items on this subject. Your computer would then tell you about all of them.) It's like your own private library.

If you'd collected a lot of other material on cars, then you could see it *all* by just typing in "CAR." Or maybe you're interested in *anything* that runs without fuel. Then you'd just type in "FUELLESS," and get back more than cars.

There are several ways in which indexing can be *built into a business.* Newspaper clippings gathered on various subjects can be sold to people who are doing research projects. Your computer does a superb job of this. Another business possibility is *abstracting the literature* in a given field. The abstract can be sold, and so can the indexes!

Some people just "take" to indexing — it's another one of those areas for unpredicted flair, just like programming. So, you mightn't have guessed what fun for *YOU* lies hidden in a computer!

So you see, your home computer can act as doorman, guard, secretary, librarian, mother's helper, consultant, new business partner, companion, and just general unpaid labor force.

BUDGET, BUDGET, WHO WANTS TO BUDGET?

A lot of people have told me that trying to set up a personal budget was no less a chore than attempting to climb Mount Everest. What's even worse is having the discipline to stay on one! Here is where a personal computer can help and pay for itself to boot.

Earlier I mentioned a checkbook balancing program. You can take this program one step further and put some limitations in. For example, you can set up a monthly accounts payable program to show a monthly debit or bill that recurs every month and channel so many dollars into it. Then when your have-to-pay bills are met, you can channel your excess to the variable type accounts. Food, entertainment, savings, and clothing accounts can be varied to a degree and you could put a dollar limit to each. When you add your check amounts into each account, your computer would let you know when you have exceeded your budget for that account.

All this sounds very formal and businesslike but let's face it, running a household is very much like running a business. Your credits to your business are your time spent at working at a job and bringing home a paycheck. Your cost of sales is your time spent away from home, expenses getting to and from work, special clothes for the job, lunches, and miscellaneous costs.

Deduct one from the other and you get a profit. From this profit you deduct your overhead expenses: rent or mortgage payments, utilities payments, automobile costs, charge accounts, food, insurance, medical payments, and loans, and what you end up with is a net profit. Hopefully this net profit is not a negative number. As you realize, too many negative numbers and you can be in deep water real quick.

A personal computer would be a very powerful tool in tackling the job of home budgeting and you could spend more of your time for leisure, rather than toiling over who's going to get what this month.

MEAL PLANNING AND KITCHEN INVENTORY

As prices keep fluctuating, and the cost of living is on the rise, a helper in the kitchen is certainly needed. A computer can offer more help in the kitchen than you think. It can't wash the dishes or scrub the floor yet, but give it time.

What this magic box can do is plan your meals for you, keep you properly rotating your canned goods and softgoods, and therefore cut down on waste. It can keep an inventory of staples and let you know when you run out or when you are overstocked.

Your computer will keep your favorite recipes at your fingertips. Using an inventory program you can plan a week's or month's meals in advance. While using existing recipes and trying new ones, you can rotate your meals and keep everyone happy by not having so many leftovers or repeating the same menu combinations too frequently.

MUSIC

One of personal computing's greatest promises is in *MUSIC.* Imagine yourself going to your piano or organ, and ***playing as slowly as you wish!*** Maybe one finger at a time, or making it up as you go. All the while, your computer is "listening." It's remembering every note. (And no one else has to hear you — you can wear headphones!)

When you're finished with your "composition," you tell your computer "play it back — to tempo." Your computer will have the piece played back, *as fast as you want it to.*

There you are. You've made your own player piano or "player organ!" And what's it playing? *YOUR* piece! Talk about *ENTERTAINMENT!!* This is an indescribable experience if you've always longed to make music, but never got the chance. *A COMPUTER IS YOUR CHANCE TO MAKE MUSIC, AT LAST — WITHOUT HAVING TO PLAY!!!*

Present-day organs are moving in this direction, but *they still require a lot of skill.* You have to be able to "keep up with the rhythm," for example. With your own computer, you won't have to, the rhythm keeps up with you.

DRAW THAT PICTURE

With the technology advancing daily, new and different applications in computer art are developing. There are graphics interface modules you can use today that allow you to draw and reproduce pictures of varied shapes and forms.

Computer art is becoming widely used among new artists who are looking for a different way of expressing themselves on paper and canvas.

Using different parameters in a software program or just letting the computer go wild have produced some of the most beautiful color combina-

tions that I have ever seen.

As you can see there is a multitude of applications for personal computers. I have touched only on a few, but you should now be able to see the tremendous impact these super machines will have on your life.

VIII.

WHAT NEXT —
A GUIDE TO YOUR GUIDES

This chapter is a reference guide for more information. If you haven't purchased your computer yet, and want to learn more about this exciting field, I have listed some monthly publications that you should pick up and clubs to visit and stores to go see. Computing is for everyone, so don't be afraid to jump in with both feet. Happy computing!

MAGAZINES

A healthy number of monthly publications have dedicated themselves to the home and hobby computer market. Purchasing a subscription to one or more of these magazines is one of the best ways to keep abreast of this ever-changing field. New developments in hardware and software are discussed in depth almost as fast as they happen.

Most of the magazines deal with a wide variety of subjects. Some pride themselves on being the leading "authority" on the subject. All of them are worth reading.

All of the following publications can be obtained at local computer stores. This is probably the best source from which to make your selection of the publications you wish to subscribe to.

Byte

Byte magazine has the largest circulation of the home computing periodicals. It was the first and boasts a circulation of over 130,000, which isn't bad for a supposed-to-be technical journal. Its articles are written by an ever-growing technical staff and also its readers.

Byte magazine is published by Byte Publications, 70 Main Street, Peterborough, New Hampshire, 03458.

Interface Age

Now, probably the fastest growing periodical, *Interface Age* magazine brings to the home and hobbyist computer user a wide variety of articles and advertisements. It started a software revolution by introducing the floppy ROM. This software media is actually a page in the magazine that is made out of plastic and is prepunched to the size of a 45 rpm record. All that is necessary to transfer its programs to a home user computer is a very simple interface, which is discussed in detail. A good software publication, *Interface Age* is published by McPheters, Wolfe, and Jones, 16704 Marquardt Avenue, Cerritos, California, 90701.

Kilobaud

This publication tries to have a blend of software and hardware articles as well as editorials of interest. It does a bang-up job of bringing this to its readers. Though not the most colorful or inventive on its jacket covers, *Kilobaud* adds a flair to its publication every month in its remarks and informative editorials. *Kilobaud* is published by Kilobaud, Petersborough, New Hampshire, 03458.

Rom

ROM is the newest in the line of home and hobby computing magazines. It brings to the reader a beginning approach to computing. An on-going section deals with buss words, and defines them very well. Some of the articles are a little too philosophical, in my book, but in any case it is a good magazine. *ROM* is published by ROM Publications Corp., Route 97, Hampton, Conn., 06247.

Personal Computing

PC is a magazine with somewhat different goals. It deals with the entire computing field. Those who use timesharing facilities, school, home, hobby, and small business computing are dealt with. *Personal Computing* is a growing publication that has a strong influence on its readers. *Personal Computing* is published by Benwell Publishing Corp., 167 Corey Road, Brookline, Mass., 02146.

Creative Computing

Another publication that lives up to its name — it does very creative work in articles on software. This bi-monthly publication has a young staff that is growing along with the magazine. It's published by Creative Computing, P.O. Box 789-M, Morristown, New Jersey, 07960.

Dr. Dobbs Journal of Computer Calisthenics and Orthodontia

A very snappy title to a magazine that carries no advertising. This publication prides itself on unbiased reviews of hardware and software on the market. Mainly software-oriented, the *Journal* gives the reader an in-depth study of the subject. Not a magazine for the beginner. Published by People's Computer Company, P.O. Box E, Menlo Park, California, 94025.

Peoples Computer

Another publication of People's Computer Company. This magazine deals with the educational marketplace. Most of its articles are aimed at teaching some of the basics of software and hardware. Most of its advisors and writers are teachers dedicated to bringing computing to the student. Again published by People's Computer Company, P.O. Box E, Menlo Park, California, 94025.

COMPUTER CLUBS

All of the clubs and groups below are bringing together people interested in computers. Attend a meeting. You will find a wealth of information and many interesting, friendly people. If there isn't a club nearby, start one yourself. It's fun!

ALABAMA

North Alabama Computer Club
c/o Jack Crenshaw
1409 Blevins Gap Road SE
Huntsville, AL 35802

CALIFORNIA

Bay Area Microprocessor Users
   Group
4565 Black Avenue
Pleasanton, CA 94566

Beverly Hills High School
   Computer Club
241 Marino Dr.
Beverly Hills, CA 90212

Computer Guild
Box 255232
Sacramento, CA 95825

Computer Organization of Los
   Angeles
P.O. Box 43677
Los Angeles, CA 90043

Computer Phreaques United
c/o Mac McCormick
2090 Cross Street
Seaside, CA 93955

Glendale Community College
   Computer Club
c/o V.X. Lashleu
1500 N. Verdugo Road
Glendale, CA 92108

Homebrew Computer Club
P.O. Box 626
Mountain View, CA 94042

Litton Calculator/Computer Club
Litton Guidance and Control
   Systems MS 78/31
5500 Canoga Ave.
Woodland Hills, CA 91364

LLLRA Hobbyist Group
c/o Charles D. Hoover
35 West Essen Street
Stockton, CA 95204

LO*OP Center
8099 La Plaza
Cotati, CA 94928

North Orange County Computer
   Club
Box 3603
Orange, CA 92665

Sacramento Minicomputer
   Users Group
Box 741
Citrus Heights, CA 95610

San Diego Computing Society
P.O. Box 9988
San Diego, CA 92109

San Gabriel SCCS
c/o Dan Erikson
400 S. Catalina Avenue
Pasadena, CA 91106

San Luis Obispo Microcomputer
   Club
439 B. Marsh St.
San Luis Obispo, CA 93401

Santa Barbara Computer Group
c/o Glenn A. McComb
210 Barrunca, Apt. 2
Santa Barbara, CA 93101

Santa Barbara Nameless
   Computer Club
c/o Doug Penrod
1445 La Clima Road
Santa Barbara, CA 93101

Southern California Computer
   Society
P.O. Box 987
South Pasadena, CA 91030

29 Palms California Area Group
c/o Sgt. Wesley Isgrigg
74055 Casita Drive
29 Palms, CA 92277

UCLA Computer Club
3514 Boelter Hall
UCLA
Los Angeles, CA 90024

Valley Chapter, SCCS
c/o R. Stuart Gibbs
5652 Lemona Ave.
Van Nuys, CA 91411

Ventura County Computer
  Society
Box 525
Port Hueneme, CA 93041

COLORADO

Denver Amateur Computer
  Society
P.O. Box 6338
Denver, Colo. 80206

CONNECTICUT

Amateur Computer Society
260 Noroton
Darien, CT 06820

Connecticut Microists
c/o George Ahmuty
6011 Wendy Lane
Westport, CT 06881

Connecticut SCCS
c/o Charles Floto
267 Willow Street
New Haven, CT 06511

U. of Hartford Microcomputer
  Club
College of Engineering — Dana
  Hall
200 Bloomfield Ave.
West Hartford, CT 06117

DISTRICT OF COLUMBIA

Washington Amateur Computer
  Society, CMC
Robert Jones
4201 Massachusetts Ave., Apt.
  168W
Washington, D.C. 20016

FLORIDA

Jacksonville Computer Club
Regency East Office Park
9951 Atlantic Blvd., Suite 326
Jacksonville, FL 32211

Miami Area Computer Club
c/o Terry Williamson
P.O. Box 430852, S.
Miami, FL 33143

Miami Computer Club
John Lynn I
13431 SW 79th
Miami, FL 33183

Miami Computer Society of
  Florida
Box 3284
Downtown Station
Tampa, FL 33604

South Florida Computer Group
410 NW 117 St.
Miami, FL 33168

Southern Florida
c/o Roberto Denis
11080 NW 39th Street
Coral Springs, FL 33065

Space Coast Microcomputer Club
c/o Ray O. Lockwood
1825 Canal Ct.
Merritt Island, FL 32952

Tallahassee Amateur Computer
   Society
c/o Larry Hughes
Rt. 14 Box 351-116
Tallahassee, FL 32304

Univ. of Florida Amateur
   Computer Society
Electrical Engineering Dept.
Rm. 234, Larson Hall
Gainesville, FL 32611

GEORGIA

Atlanta Area Microcomputer
   Club
c/o Jim Dunion
421 Ridgecrest Road
Atlanta, GA 30307

Atlanta Area Microcomputer
   Hobbyist Group
Box 33140
Atlanta, GA 30332

HAWAII

Aloha Computer Club
c/o Robert Kennedy
1541 Dominus No. 1404
Honolulu, HI 96822

ILLINOIS

Chicago Area Computer
   Hobbyist's Exchange (CACHE)
P.O. Box 36
Vernon Hill, IL 60061

Altair-Chicago
517 Talcott Rd.
Park Ridge, IL 60068

Chicago Area Microcomputer
   Users Group
c/o Bill Precht
1102 S. Edison
Lombard, IL 60148

IDAHO

CSPCC
c/o Mark Bentley
205 Foster, Apt. 2
Coeur d'Alene, ID 83814

INDIANA

Beta Iota Tau
c/o Richard R. Petke
R.H.I.T. Box 420
Terre Haute, IN 47803

Bloomington Association for
   the Computer Sciences
c/o Remy M. Simpson
901 East 13th St.
Bloomington, IN 47401

Hoosier Amateur Computer and
   Kluge Society
c/o Ray Borill
111 S. College Ave.
Bloomington, IN 47401

Indiana Small Systems Group
54 Sherry Lane
Brownsburg, IN 46112

Louisville Area Users of
   Microprocessors
115 Edgemont Drive
New Albany, IN 47150

Purdue University Computer
   Hobbyist Club (PUNCH)
Rm.67, Electrical Engineering
   Bldg.
Purdue University
West Lafayette, IN 47907

IOWA

Eastern Iowa Computer Club
c/o Mike Wimble
6026 Underwood Ave. SW
Cedar Rapids, IA 52404

KANSAS

Computer Network of Kansas
City
c/o Earl Day
968 Kansas Ave.
Kansas City, KS 66105

South Central Kansas Amateur
Computer Association
c/o Cris Borger
1504 N. St. Clair
Wichita, KS 67203

KENTUCKY

Louisville Area Users of
Microprocessors
c/o Steve Roberts (Cybertronics)
P.O. Box 18065
Louisville, KY 40218

LOUISIANA

New Orleans Computer Club
Emile Alline
1119 Pennsylvania Ave.
Slidell, LA 70458

MASSACHUSETTS

Alcove Computer Club
c/o John P. Vullo
21 Sunset Ave.
North Reading, MA 01864

Greater Boston Computer Users
Group
c/o Steven Hain
40 Wilshire Drive (Door 2)
Sharon, MA 02067

New England Computer Society
P.O. Box 198
Bedford, MA 01730

MICHIGAN

Ann Arbor Computing Club
c/o Roger Gregory
1485 Newport Road
Ann Arbor, MI 48103

C.J. Lamesfield
Box 271
Davison, MI 48423

Computer Hobbyists Around
Lansing
c/o Joyce and Marvin Church
4307 Mar Moor Drive
Lansing, MI 48917

Detroit Area Club
c/o Dennis Siemit
45466 Cluster
Utica, MI 48087

Detroit Area Users Group
c/o Dana Badertscher
18300 Ash
East Detroit, MI 48021

Mid-Michigan Computer Group
c/o Tony Preston
15151 Ripple Dr.
Linden, MI 48451

MINNESOTA

Bit Users Association
Resources Access Center
3010 4th Avenue S.
Minneapolis, MN 55408

Minnesota Computer Society
c/o Jean Rice
Box 35317
Minneapolis, MN 55435

Southern Minnesota Amateur
Computer Club
2212 NW 17th Ave.
Rochester, MN 55901

NEVADA

Northern Nevada Amateur
  Computer Club
UNSCC
Box 9068
Reno, NV 89507

NEW HAMPSHIRE

Nashua Area Computer Club
c/o Dwayne Jeffries
181 Cypress Lane
Nashua, NH 03060

NEW JERSEY

Amateur Computer Group
  of New Jersey
c/o Sol Libes
UCTI
1776 Raritan Road
Scotch Plains, NJ 07076

Holmdel Microprocessor Club
c/o Fred Horney
Rm. 3D317
Bell Telephone Labs
Holmdel, NJ 07733

New Jersey Club
c/o Bruce C. Dalland
37 Brook Drive
Dover, NJ 07801

Northern New Jersey Amateur
  Computer Group
c/o Murray P. Dwight
593 New York Ave.
Lyndhurst, NJ 07071

NEW MEXICO

Albuquerque Area Computer
  Club
Gary Tack
P.O. Box 866
Corrales, NM 87048

NEW YORK

Buffalo Club
c/o Chuck Fischer
355 South Creek Drive
Depew, NY 14043

Ithaca Computer Club
c/o Steve Edelman
204 Dryden Road
Ithaca, NY 14850

Long Island Computer
  Association
c/o Gary Harrison
P.O. Box 864
Jamaica, NY 11431

Long Island Computer Club
c/o Popular Electronics
One Park Avenue
New York, NY 10016

New York Amateur Computer
  Club
106 Bedford St.
New York, NY 10014

New York Micro Hobbyist Group
c/o Robert Schwartz
375 Roverside Drive, Apt. 1E
New York, NY 10025

Stony Brook Home-Brew
  Computer Club
c/o Ludwig Braun
College of Engineering and
  Applied Sciences
State University of NY at
  Stony Brook
Stony Brook, NY 11794

Niagara Region Computer Group
c/o Chuck Fischer
355 South Creek Drive
Depew, NY 14043

110

Rochester Area Microcomputer
Society (RAMS)
Box D
Rochester, NY 14609

Students Cybernetics Lab
16 Linwood Ave.
Buffalo, NY 14209

Westchester Amateur Computer
Society
c/o Harold Chair
41 Colby Avenue
Rye, NY 10580

Westchester Fairfield Amateur
Computer Society
RR 1 Box 198
Pound Ridge, NY 10576

NORTH CAROLINA

Triangle Amateur Computer Club
Box 17523
Raleigh, NC 27609

OHIO

Amateur Computer Society of
Columbus
c/o Walter Marvin
408 Thurber Drive West No. 6
Columbus, OH 43215

Cleveland Digital Group
c/o John Kabat, Jr.
1200 Seneca Blvd. No. 407
Broadway Heights, OH 44147

Dayton Microcomputer Assn.
c/o Doug Andrews
8668 Sturbridge Avenue
Cincinnati, OH 45200

Compute, Evaluate, Trade
Box 104
Tipp City, Oh 45371

Midwest Alliance of Computer
Clubs
c/o Gary Coleman
P.O. Box 83
Brecksville, OH 44141

OKLAHOMA

Central Oklahoma Amateur
Computing Society
c/o Lee Lilly
P.O. Box 2213
Norman, OK 73069

Oklahoma City Club
c/o Bill Cowden
2412 SW 45th
Oklahoma City, OK 73119

OREGON

Portland Computer Club
c/o Bill Marsh
2814 NE 40th Street
Portland, OR 97212

Portland Computer Society
1003 Garland St. Apt. 4
Woodburn, OR 97071

PENNSYLVANIA

Delaware Valley Chapter, SCCE
c/o Martin Dimmerman
1228 Barrowdale
Rydal, PA 19046

Philadelphia Area
Computer Society
Box 1954
Philadelphia, PA 19105

Pittsburgh Area Computer Club
c/o Fred Kitman
OPUS-1
400 Smithfield Road
Pittsburgh, PA 15222

Saint Thomas District High
   School Computer Club
1025 Braddock Ave.
Braddock, PA 15104

Wilkes College Computer Club
c/o Erick Jansen, Math Dept.
Wilkes College
Wilkes-Barre, PA 18703

TEXAS

Central Texas Computer
   Association
c/o Ray McCoy
508 Blueberry Hill
Austin, TX 78745

El Paso Computer Group
c/o Jack O. Coats, Jr.
213 Argonaut Apt. 27
El Paso, TX 79912

Houston Amateur
   Microcomputer Club
   (HAMCC)
c/o David M. Fogg
4223 S. W. Freeway No. 203
Houston, TX 77207

NASA-JSC Computer Hobbyist
   Club
c/o Marlowe Cassetti
1011 Davenport
Seabrook, TX 77586

Northside Computer Group
2318 Townbreeze
San Antonio, TX 78238

Panhandle Computer Society
c/o Tex Evertt
2923 S. Spring
Amarillo, TX 79103

Permian Basin Computer Group
c/o John Rabenaldt
Ector County School District
Box 3912
Odessa, TX 79760

Texas A & M University
   Microcomputer Club
P.O. Box M-9
Aggieland Station, TX 77844

Texas Computer Club
c/o L.G. Walker
Rt. 1, Box 272
Aledo, TX 76008

The Computer Hobbyist Group
   of North Texas
c/o Bill Fuller
2377 Dalworth 157
Grand Prairie, TX 75050

UTAH

Salt Lake City Computer Club
2925 Valley View Avenue
Holladay, UT 84117

VIRGINIA

Alexandria Chapter, CMC
c/o Richard Rubinstein
7711 Elba Road
Alexandria, VA 22306

Charlottesville Computer
   Hobbyist Club
Box 6132
Charlottesville, VA 22906

Dyna-Micro Users Group
c/o Dr. Frank Settle, Jr.
Digital Directions
P.O. Box 1053
Lexington, VA 24450

112

Peninsula Computer
   Hobbyist Club
c/o Larry Polis
2 Weber Lane
Hampton, VA 23663

Roanoke Valley Computer Club
c/o Lee Yosafat
2026 Wynmere Drive SW
Roanoke, VA

WASHINGTON

Northwest Computer Club
P.O. Box 5304
Seattle, WA

Northwest Computer Club
P.O. Box 5304
Seattle, WA 98105

WISCONSIN

Durant Club
c/o James S. White
901 South 12th St.
Watertown, WI 53094

Wisconsin Area Tribe of
   Computer Hobbyists
   (WATCH)
c/o Don Stevens
P.O. Box 159
Sheboygan Falls, WI 53085

CANADA

Amateur Microprocessor Club
   of Kitchner-Waterloo
c/o Ed Spike
Electrical Engineering
University of Waterloo
Waterloo, Ontario N2L 3G1

Canadian Computer Club
861 111th St.
Brandon, Manitoba R7A 4L1
Montreal Area Computer Society
c/o Leslie Zoltan
4100 Kindersley Ave. Apt. 22
Montreal, Quebec

Toronto Region of
   Computer Enthusiasts
   (TRACE)
c/o Harold G. Melanson
Box 545
Streetsville, Ontario L5M 2C1

COMPUTER STORES

Computer stores are the biggest influence on the home computer market today because they bring to the public a hands-on opportunity to explore the field. The first computer store was opened in August 1975 in Santa Monica, California. Today there are over 500 and still coming.

Most computer retail stores sell a variety of products. Some are devoted to special lines, while others give a wide choice. What computer stores can offer besides the equipment they sell is the basic support every new home computer owner needs, software. The only limitation of any of the home computers on the marketplace today is what the user hasn't dreamed up yet. Your local computer store is a vast resource of software support. They sell and maintain numerous programs to put your computer to.

Not only does the store give you support in software, but it maintains the

113

hardware as well. Sooner or later there is a hardware breakdown. Instead of sending your equipment back to the manufacturer, your local store can repair and maintain it for you.

Visit them and ask questions. The storekeepers are very helpful and should open up their knowledge and experience to you. They want to have you as a customer now and in the future.

ALABAMA

COMPUTER CENTER
OF BIRMINGHAM
303-B Poplar Pl.
Birmingham, AL 35209

I.C.P., COMPUTER LAND
1550 Montgomery Highway
Birmingham, AL 35226

COMPUTER LAND
3020 University Drive
Huntsville, AL 35805

ARIZONA

BITS & BYTES COMPUTER
SHOP
2380 W. Betty Elyse Ln.
Phoenix, AZ 85023

ARIZONA MICRO SYSTEMS
3240 W. Larkspur Dr.
Phoenix, AZ 85029

PERSONAL COMPUTER
PLACE
1840 W. Southern
Mesa, AZ 85202

BYTE SHOP — EAST
803 N. Scottsdale Rd.
Tempe, AZ 85281

TRI-TEK, INC.
6522 N. 43rd Ave.
Glendale, AZ 85301

ALTAIR COMPUTER
CENTER
4941 E. 29th St.
Tucson, AZ 85711

BYTE SHOP OF TUCSON
2612 E. Broadway
Tucson, AZ 85716

ARKANSAS

COMPUTER PRODUCTS
UNLTD.
4216 W. 12th St.
Little Rock, AR 72204

COMPUTER PRODS. UNLTD.
2412 S. Broadway
Little Rock, AR 72206

COMP STORE — NIEMEYER
FEED
4818 Asher Box 4045
Little Rock, AR 72214

CALIFORNIA

BYTE WESTWOOD
1762 Westwood Blvd.
Westwood, CA 90024

BYTE WESTCHESTER
8711 La Tierra Ave.
Westchester, CA 90045

COMPUTER LAND
16919 Hawthorne Ave.
Lawndale, CA 90260

COMPUTER STORE
820 Broadway
Santa Monica, CA 90401

MISSION CONTROL
2008 Wilshire Blvd.
Santa Monica, CA 90403

MICRO COMPUTER STORE
9323 Warbler Ave.
Fountain Valley, CA 92708

MICRO COMPUTERS
18120 Brookhurst
Fountain Valley, CA 92708

CUSTOM COMPUTER
SYSTEMS
11 Creekside
Irvine, CA 92715

MICROCOMPUTER CENTER
1211 S. Western #a
Anaheim, CA 92805

ALGORITHM — COMPUTER
STORE
2330 Harbor Blvd.
Costa Mesa, CA 92606

COMPUTER CENTER
1913 Harbor Blvd.
Costa Mesa, CA 92627

COMPUTER WAY
15525 Computer Lane
Huntington Beach, CA 92649

COMPUTER MART OF
ORANGE COUNTY
625 W. Katella #10
Orange, CA 92667

BYTE SHOP —
PLACENTIA
123 E. Yorba Linda Blvd.
Placentia, CA 92670

COMPUTERWARE
380 1st St.
Encinitas, CA 92042

BYTE SHOP — SAN DIEGO
8250-H Vickers St.
San Diego, CA 92111

COMPUTER CENTER OF SAN
DIEGO
8205 Ronson Road
San Diego, CA 92111

COMPUTERLAND
4233 Convoy St.
San Diego, CA 92111

SAN DIEGO COMPUTER
CENTER
8250 Vickers Road
San Diego, CA 92111

COMPUTER COMPONENTS
INC.
5848 Sepulveda Blvd.
Van Nuys, CA 91411

PEOPLE'S COMPUTER SHOP
13452 Ventura Blvd.
Sherman Oaks, CA 91423

BYTE SHOP OF BURBANK
1812 W. Burbank Blvd.
Burbank, CA 91506

TECH-MART
19590 Ventura Blvd.
Tarzana, CA 91536

COMPUTER POWER AND
LIGHT CO.
12321 Ventura Blvd.
Studio City, CA 91604

DATA BUS
354 Springfield St.
Claremont, CA 91711

SUNSHINE COMPUTER CO.
20710 S. Leapwood Ave.
Carson, CA 90749

A-VIDD ELECTRONICS CO.
2110 Bellflower Blvd.
Long Beach, CA 90815

BYTE SHOP — LONG BEACH
5453 E. Stearns St.
Long Beach, CA 90815

BYTE SHOP OF PASADENA
496 S. Lake Ave.
Pasadena, CA 91101

BYTE SHOP OF LAWNDALE
16508 Hawthorne Blvd.
Lawndale, CA 90260

BITS, BYTES & PIECES
6211 Quincewood Cir.
Citrus Heights, CA 95610

BYTE SHOP OF CITRUS
HEIGHTS
6041 Greenback Lane
Citrus Heights, CA 95610

BYTE SHOP OF BERKELEY
1514 University Ave.
Berkeley, CA 94703

COMPUTER KITS, INC.
1044 University Ave.
Berkeley, CA 94710

BYTE SHOP OF SAN RAFAEL
509 B. Francisco Blvd.
San Rafael, CA 94901

COMPUTER CENTER
1801 E. Cotati Ave.
Rohnert Park, CA 94928

BYTE SHOP OF DIABLO
VALLEY
2989 N. Main
Walnut Creek, CA 94956

COMPUTER TERMINAL
209 S. San Mateo Dr.
San Mateo, CA 94401

BYTE SHOP OF SAN MATEO
1200 W. Hillsdale Blvd.
San Mateo, CA 94403

BYTE SHOP OF HAYWARD
1122 B. St.
Hayward, CA 94541

COMPUTERLAND OF
HAYWARD
22634 Foothill Blvd.
Hayward, CA 94541

BYTE OF PALO ALTO
2233 El Camino Real
Palo Alto, CA 94302

BYTE SHOP OF SANTA
CLARA
3400 El Camino Real
Santa Clara, CA 95050

RECREATIONAL COMPUTER
CENTER
1324 S. Mary Ave.
Sunnyvale, CA 94087

COMPUTER STORE OF
SAN FRANCISCO
1093 Mission St.
San Francisco, CA 94103

BYTE SHOP OF SAN
FRANCISCO
321 Pacific Ave
San Frandisco, CA 94111

SMALL BUSINESS
COMPUTER CO.
400 Dewey Blvd.
San Francisco, CA 94116

BYTE SHOP OF
MT. VIEW
1063 El Camino Real
Mt. View, CA 94040

DIGITAL DELI
80 W. El Camino Real
Mountain View, CA 94040

BYTE SHOP OF
SANTA BARBARA
4 W. Mission St.
Santa Barbara, CA 93101

BYTE SHOP SAN FERNANDO
18424 Ventura Blvd.
Tarzana, CA 91356

BYTE SHOP THOUSAND
OAKS
2705 Thousand Oaks Blvd.
Thousand Oaks, CA 93160

PROKO ELECTRONICS
SHOPPE
439-B Marsh St.
San Luis Obispo, CA 93401

COMPUTER CENTER
1913 Harbor Blvd.
Costa Mesa, CA 93626

BYTE SHOP OF FRESNO
3141 E. McKinley
Fresno, CA 93703

COMPUTERLAND OF
SADDLEBACK VALLEY
24001 Via Fabricanted
Mission Viejo, CA 92675

COMPUTERLAND OF
TUSTIN
101 W. 1st St.
Tustin, CA 92680

BYTE SHOP OF
WESTMINSTER
14300 Beach Blvd.
Westminster, CA 92683

COMPUTER EMPORIUM
2082 SE Briston #11
Newport Beach, CA 92707

BYTE SHOP OF SANTA
CLARA
3400 El Camino Real
Santa Clara, CA 95051

COMPUTER ROOM OF
SAN JOSE
124-H Blossom Hill Rd.
San Jose, CA 95123

BYTE SHOP OF SAN JOSE
2626 Union
San Jose, CA 95124

MICROCOMPUTER APPLIC
SYS
2322 Capitol Ave.
Sacramento, CA 95816

BYTE OF STOCKTON
5518 Florin Road
Sacramento, CA 95823

COMPUTER WORLD STORE
1309 Court St.
Redding, CA 96001

COLORADO

SMITH SYSTEMS ASSOC.
1221 S. Clarkson #122
Denver, CO 80210

GATEWAY ELECTRONICS
2839 W. 44th Ave.
Denver, CO. 80211

COMPUTER COUNTRY, INC.
1800 Alameda Sq.
2200 W. Alameda
Denver, CO 80223

BYTE SHOP OF BOULDER
2040-30th St.
Boulder, CO 80301

INTERMOUNTAIN DIGITAL
1027 Dellwood Ave.
Boulder, CO 80302

POOR RICHARDS
CALCULATOR CO.
204 W. Laurel St.
Ft. Collins, CO 80521

BYTE SHOP OF ENGLEWOOD
3464 S. Acoma
Englewood, CO 80110

BYTE OF ARAPAHOE
COUNTY
3264 S. Acoma
Englewood, CO 80110

COMPUTER HUT OF
DENVER
1764 Blake St.
Denver, CO 80202

CONNECTICUT

HEURISTIC SYSTEMS
244 Crystal Lake Rd.
Ellington, CT 06029

COMPUTER STORE OF
CONNECTICUT
63 South Main St.
Windsor Locks, CT 06096

COMPUTERLAND OF
FAIRFIELD
2475 Blackrock Turnpike
Fairfield, CT 06430

COMPUTER MART
965 Bixwell Avenue
Hamden, CT 06514

RADIO COMMUNICATION
SERVICE
24 Rockdale Rd.
West Haven, CT 06516

JRV COMPUTER STORE
3714 Whitney Avenue
Hamden, CT 06518

ELECTRONIC MARKETING
CO.
1092 Jonson Rd.
Woodbridge, CT 06525

KAUFMAN ELECTRONICS
INC.
73 Frank St.
Bridgeport, CT 06604

COMPUTER WORLD
3876 Main St.
Bridgeport, CT 06606

TECHNOLOGY SYSTEMS
20 Chestnut St.
Bethel, CT 06801

FINANCIAL COMPUTER ST.
1234 Summer St.
Stamford, CT 06905

DELAWARE

COMPUTER GENERAL
STORE
1206 Flint Hill Road
Wilmington, DE 19808

COMPUTERLAND
3011 Ridgevale
Wilmington, DE 19808

ARTIFICIAL INTELLIGENCE
3308 Altamont Dr.
Wilmington, DE 19810

WASHINGTON DC

GEORGETOWN COMP.
EMPORIUM
3268 M Street
NW Washington, DC 20007

FLORIDA

COMPUTER EQUIPMENT
SALES CO.
1525 SE 15th St.
Ft. Lauderdale, FL 33316

BYTE SHOP
1044 E. Oakland Pk. Blvd.
Ft. lauderdale, FL 33334

COMPUTER STORE
1549 W. Branden Blvd.
Brandon, FL 33511

ELECON CORP.
COMPUTER STORE
4981-72nd Ave. N.
Pinellas Park, FL 33565

MICROCOMPUTER
SYSTEMS, INC.
144 S. Dale Mabry Hwy.
Tampa, FL 33609

MARSH DATA SYSTEMS
5405-B Southern Comfort
Tampa, FL 33614

BYTE SHOP — COCOA
BEACH
1325 N. Atlantic Ave.
Cocoa Beach, FL 32931

SUNNY COMPUTER STORES,
INC.
117 Newton Rd.,
W. Hollywood, FL 33023

MICRO COMPUTER SYSTEM
6492 SW 8th Ct.
Pompano Beach, FL 33068

AMATEUR RADIO CENTER,
INC.
2805 NE 2nd Ave.
Miami, FL 33137

ELECTRONIC EQUIP CO.
INC.
4027 NW 24th St.
Miami, FL 33142

SUNNY COMPUTER STORES,
INC.
1238A S. Dixie Hwy.
Coral Gables, FL 33146

BYTE SHOP OF MIAMI
7825 Bird Road
Miami, FL 33155

THE COMPUTER STORE
623 University Blvd.
N. Jacksonville, FL 32211

DOUGLAS COMPUTER
SYSTEMS
710 Oaks Plantation Dr.
Jacksonville, FL 32211

COMPUTER STORE OF
PENSACOLA
3804 N. 9th Ave.
Pensacola, FL 32503

DATA ENTRY ENGINEERING
1810 N. Orange Ave.
Orlando, FL 32804

GEORGIA

ATLANTA COMPUTER
MART
5091 B. Buford Hwy.
Atlanta, GA 30340

HAWAII

MICROCOMPUTER SYSTEMS
OF HAWAII
Kukui Plaza
1248 Pali Hwy.
Honolulu, HI 96813

119

SMALL COMPUTER
SYSTEMS
3140 Waialae Ave.
Honolulu, HI 96816

ILLINOIS

ACRO ELECTRONICS CORP.
1101 W. Chicago Ave. E.
Chicago, IL 46312

COMPUTERLAND
50 E. Rand Rd.
Arlington Heights, IL 60004

CURTIS ENTERPRISES
1220 Winwood Dr.
Lake Forest, IL 60045

CHICAGO COMPUTER
STORE
517 Talcott Rd./Hwy. 62
Park Ridge, IL 60068

LILLIPUTE COMPUTER
MART
4046 Oakton St.
Skokie, IL 60076

CONTEMPORARY MKT, INC.
790 Maple Lane
Bensenville, IL 60106

MPU SHOP
195 Spangler Ave.
Elmhurst, IL 60126

ITTY BITTY MACHINE CO.
42 W. Roosevelt
Lombard, IL 60148

GEORGE ELECTRONICS INC.
325 E. 147th St.
Harvey, IL 60426

BITS & BYTES COMPUTER
STORE
W. 147th St. Box G 2928
Posen, IL 60469

CREATIVE ELECTRONICS
600 Enterprise Dr. #203
Oakbrook, IL 60521

ASPEN COMPUTERS INC.
7519 W. Irving Park
Chicago, IL 60634

JOSEPH ELECTRONICS INC.
8830 Milwaukee Ave.
Niles, IL 60648

IMPERIAL COMP. SYSTEMS,
INC.
2105 23rd Ave.
Rockford, IL 61101

CHAMPAIGN COMPUTER CO.
318 N. Hickory
Champaign, IL 61820

DIGITAL RESEARCH
311 E. White, RM 33
Champaign, IL 61820

NUMBERS RACKET
318 E. Green St.
Champaign, Il 61820

THE COMPUTER STORE
OF CHAMPAIGN
#2 Woodbine
Mahumet, IL 61853

INDIANA

HOME COMPUTER CENTER
2115 E. 62nd St.
Indianapolis, IN 46220

HOME COMPUTER SHOP
10447 Chris Dr.
Indianapolis, IN 46229

DATA GROUP, INC. —
BYTE SHOP
5947 E. 82nd St.
Indianapolis, IN 46250

COMPUTERS UNLIMITED
7724 E. 89th St.
Indianapolis, IN 46256

QUANTUM COMPUTER
WORKS
6637 Kennedy Ave.
Hammond, IN 46323

THE DATA DOMAIN OF
FORT WAYNE
2805 E. State Blvd.
Fort Wayne, IN 46805

DATA DOMAIN
406 S. College
Bloomington, IN 47401

CASTRUPS RADIO SUPPLIES
1014 W. Franklin St.
Evansville, IN 47710

DATA DOMAIN OF W.
LAFAYETTE
219 W. Columbia W.
Lafayette, IN 47904

COMPUTER SPECIALIST
107 N. Chauncey
W. Lafayette, IN 47906

IOWA
RADIO TRADE SUPPLY CO.
1013-1017 High St.
Des Moines, IA 50309

MIDWEST COMPUTER
STORE
4005 Ninth St.
Des Moines, IA 50313

MICRO BUS INC.
1910 Mt. Vernon Rd. SE
Cedar Rapids, IA 54203

COMPUTER STORE OF
DAVENPORT
616 W. 35th St.
Davenport, IA 62806

KANSAS

KANSAS CITY CALIBRATION
968 Kansas Ave.
Kansas City, KS 66105

BYTE OF MISSION
5809 W. 101st St.
Overland Park, KS 66209

HOBBY HAVEN
Metcalf S. Shop Ctr.
Overland Park, KS 66212

AMAT RADIO EQUIP CO.
INC.
1203 E. Douglas
Wichita, KS 67211

COMPUTERLAND
1262 N. Hillside
Wichita, KS 67214

COMPUTER SYSTEMS
DESIGN
1611 E. Central
Wichita, KS 67214

KENTUCKY

LOGIC SYSTEMS
324 W. Woodlawn Ave.
Louisville, KY 40214

DATA DOMAIN OF
LOUISVILLE
3028 Hunsinger Lane
Louisville, Ky 402220

COMPUTERLAND OF
LOUISVILLE
813B Lyndon Lane
Louisville, KY 40222

CYBERTRONICS, INC.
312 Productions Ct.
Louisville, KY 40299

121

DATA DOMAIN OF
LEXINGTON
506½ Euclid Ave.
Lexington, KY 40501

LOUISIANA

TRIONICS
725 Focis Metarie
Metarie, LA 70005

ALTAIR COMPUTER
CENTER
8610 Oak St.
New Orleans, LA 70118

THE COMPUTER SHOPPE
344 Camp New Orleans, LA
New Orleans, LA 70130

EXECUTONE
MICROCOMPUTER
6969 Titian Ave.
Baton Rouge, LA 70809

SOUTHERN ELECTRONICS
INC.
2422 Southern Ave.
Shreveport, LA 71104

MARYLAND

COMM CENTER
9624 Ft. Meade Rd.
Laurel, MD 20810

COMPUTERLAND OF
ROCKVILLE
16065 Frederick Dr.
Rockville, MD 20850

COMPUTER WORKSHOP OF
DC
11308 Hounds Way
Rockville, MD 20852

COMPUTERS, ETC.
13A Allegheny Ave.
Townson, MD 21204

AMER DISTRIBUTING
COMPANY
4531 Baltimore Ntl. Pike
Baltimore, MD 21228

MASSACHUSETTS

MICROTEC
23 Hamburg St.
Springfield, MA 01107

COMPUTER STORE
OF BURLINGTON
120 Cambridge St..
Burlington, MA 01803

B & F ENTERPRISES
119 Foster St.
Peabody, MA 01960

COM SHOP — AIR COM
CORP.
288 Norfolk St.
Cambridge, MA 02139

CPU SHOP
41 Pleasant St.
Charlestown, MA 02145

COMPUTER MART, INC.
473 Winter St.
Waltham, MA 02154

COMPUTER MART OF MASS.
1097 Lexington
Waltham, MA 02154

TUFTS RADIO
ELECTRONICS
209 Mystic Ave.
Medford, MA 02155

ICA
30 Park Ave.
Arlington, MA 02174

AMERICAN USED
COMPUTER CORP.
412 Beacon St.
Boston, MA 02215

COMPUTER WAREHOUSE
584 Commonwealth Ave.
Boston, MA 02215

MICHIGAN
PURCHASE RADIO SUPPLY
327 E. Hoover
Ann Arbor, MI 48104

LUMEN COMPUTER
EXCHANGE
1250 N. Main St.
Ann Arbor, MI 48107

COMPUTER STORE
310 E. Washington St.
Ann Arbor, MI 48108

NORTHWEST ELECTRONICS
33610 Plymouth Rd.
Livonia, MI 48150

SMALL SCALE SYSTEMS
13003 Ostrander Road
Maybee, MI 48159

HOBBY HOUSE
1035 W. Territorial Rd.
Battle Creek, MI 49015

ELECT. DISTRIBUTORS, INC.
1960 Peck St.
Muskegon, MI 49441

RADIO PARTS, INC.
542-548 S. Div. Ave.
Grand Rapids, MI 49502

COMPUTER MART, INC.
1800 W. 14 MI Rd.
Royal Oak, MI 48073

COMPUTER SYSTEMS
26401 Harper St.
Clair Shores, MI 48081

GENERAL COMPUTER
STORE
2011 Livernois
Troy, MI 48084

COMPUMART, INC.
1250 North Main St.
Ann Arbor, MI 48104

NEWMAN COMPUTER
EXCHANGE
3960 Varsity Drive
Ann Arbor, MI 48104

MINNESOTA

BYTE SHOP MINNESOTA
7545 Irish Ave.
Cottage Grove, MN 55016

BYTE SHOP OF EAGAN
1434 Yankee Doodle Road
Eagan, MN 55121

COMPUTER ROOM OF ST.
PAUL
3938 Beau D'Rue Dr.
St. Paul, MN 55122

BYTE SHOP OF
EAGAN MICROPROGRAM-
MING, INC.
12033 Riverwood Dr.
Burnsville, MN 55337

ELECT. CENTER COMM. DIV.
127 3rd Ave. N
Minneapolis, MN 55401

COMPUTER DEPOT, INC.
1716 Midwest Plaza Bldg.
Minneapolis, MN 55402

COMPUTER DEPOT, INC.
3515 W. 70th St.
Edina, MN 55435

MISSOURI

COMPUTER WORKSHOP OF
K.C.
6903 Blair Rd.
Kansas City, Mo 64152

COMPUTER SYSTEMS
CENTER
13461 Olive Blvd.
Chesterfield, MO 63017

GATEWAY ELECTRONICS,
INC.
8123-25 Page Blvd.
St. Louis, MO 63130

MONTANA

MONTANA COMPUTER
CENTER
2512 Grand Ave.
Billings, MT 59102

ELECTRIC CITY RADIO SUP.
2315 10th Ave. S.
Great Falls, MT 59405

NEBRASKA

OMAHA COMPUTER STORE
4540 S. 84th St.
Omaha, NE 68127

ALTAIR COMPUTER
CENTER
611 N. 27th St., Suite 9
Lincoln, NE 68503

NEVADA

CENTURY 23
4566 Spring Mountain Rd.
Las Vegas, NV 89102

JOHNSON TV, INC.
2607 E. Charleston
Las Vegas, NV 89104

NEW HAMPSHIRE

WORLDWIDE
ELECTRONICS INC.
10 Flagstone Dr.
Hudson, NH 03051

COMPUTERLAND —
NASHUA
419 Amherst St.
Nashua, NH 03060

COMPUTER MART OF NH
170 Main St.
Nashua, NH 03060

MICROCOMPUTERS, INC.
539 Amhurst St.
Nashua, NH 03060

G. PAULSEN CO.
27 Sheep Davis Rd.
Concord, NH 03301

AIRCOM, INC. COMPUTER
SHOP DIV.
Route 16B
Union, NH 03887

NEW JERSEY

HOBOKEN COMPUTER
WORKS
20 Hudson Place
Hoboken, NJ 07030

RACHLES INC.
364 Oak St.
Passaic, NJ 07055

NIDISCO INC.
2812 Kennedy Blvd.
Union City, NJ 07087

MIDWEST ENTERPRISES,
INC.
815 Standish Ave.
Westfield, NJ 07090

COMPUTER CORNER OF N.J.
240 Wanague Ave.
Pompton Lakes, NJ 07742

COMPUTER ROOM OF
HACKENSACK
451 Simons Ave.
Hackensack, NJ 07601

LASHEN ELECTRONICS INC.
21 Broadway
Denville, NJ 07834

MINI COMPUTER SUPPLIER
25 Chattom Road
Summit, NJ 07901

COMPUTERLAND OF
MORRISTOWN
2 De Hart St.
Morristown, NJ 07960

WILLIAM ELECTRONICS
SUPPLY
1863 Woodbridge Ave.
Edison, NJ 08817

COMPUTER MART OF
NEW JERSEY
501 Rte. 27
Iselin, NJ 08830

MOONBEAM ELECTRONICS
205 Willow Ave.
Piscataway, NJ 08854

NEW MEXICO

COMPUTER SHACK
3120 San Mateo NE
Albuquerque, NM 87106

NEW YORK

WACO TRADING CO. INC.
239 Park Ave. S.
New York, NY 10003

DALE ELECTRONICS
244 W. 14th St.
New York, NY 10011

AUDIO DESIGN
ELECTRONICS
487 Broadway #512
New York, NY 10013

COMPUTER MART OF NEW
YORK
118 Madison Ave.
New York, NY 10016

COMPUTER STORE OF NEW
YORK
55 W. 39th St.
New York, NY 10018

ATLAS ELECTRONICS CORP.
1570 3rd Ave.
New York, NY 10028

HARVEY RADIO CO. INC.
23 W. 45th St.
New York, NY 10036

THE COMPUTER TREE, INC.
409 Hooper Road
Endwell, NY 13706

MICRO WORLD
435 Main St.
Johnson City, NY 13790

COLLEGIATE AUDIO
2-A Telfort St.
Onfonta, NY 13820

COMPUT-O-MAT
41 Colby Ave.
Rye, NY 10580

COMPUTER CORNER
White Plains Mall
200 Hamilton Ave.
White Plains, NY 10601

COMPUTER MICROSYSTEMS
6 Wooleys Lane
Great Neck, NY 11023

COMPUTER MICROSYSTEMS
1309 Northern Blvd.
Manhasset, NY 11030

SYNCHRO-SOUND
ENTERPRISES
193-25 Jamaica
Hollis, NY 11423

ELECTRONIC PRODUCTS
645 Stewart Ave.
Garden City, NY 11530

COMPUTER MART OF
LONG ISLAND
2072 Front St. E. Meadow,
Long Island, NY 11554

HARRISON RADIO
20 Smith St.
Farmingdale, NY 11735

BYTE SHOP EAST, INC.
27-21 Hempstead Turnpike
Levittown, L.I., NY 11756

SUMMIT DISTRIBUTORS,
INC.
916 Main St.
Buffalo, NY 14202

READOUT COMPUTER
STORE
6 Winspear Ave.
Buffalo, NY 14214

HOME COMPUTER CENTERS
671 Monroe Ave.
Rochester, NY 14607

COMPUTER HOUSE, INC.
721 Atlantic Avenue
Rochester, NY 14609

COMPUWORLD, INC.
2930 W. Henrietta Rd.
Rochester, NY 14623

THE MEMORY MERCHANTS
INC.
1350 Buffalo Road, Ste. 11
Rochester, NY 14624

COMPUTER LAND OF
ITHACA
225 Elmira Rd.
Ithaca, NY 14850

ITHACA AUDIO
410 College Ave. #417
Ithaca, NY 14850

CHEMUNG ELECTRONICS
INC.
601 E. Church St.
Elmira, NY 14901

THE COMPUTER SHOPPE
385 Swezey Lane
Middle Island, NY 11953

ROSE BUSINESS SYTEMS
Head-of-Pond Road
Water Mill, NY 11976

ADIRONDACK RADIO
SUPPLY
185 W. Main St.
Amsterdam, NY 12010

TROJAN ELECTRONIC
SUPPLY CO.
15 Middleburgh St.
Troy, NY 12181

FORT ORANGE
ELECTRONICS
904 Broadway
Albany, NY 12207

COMPUTER STORE, INC.
269 Osborne Rd.
Albany, NY 12211

COMPUTER SHOP OF
SYRACUSE
3307 Erie Blvd.
Dewitt, NY 13214

NORTH CAROLINA

COMPUTER ELECTRONICS
504 Carriage Lane
Cary, NC 27511

DIXIE COMPUTERS, INC.
2911 Essex Cir.
Glenwood V
Raleigh, NC 27608

COMPUTER ASSOCIATES,
INC.
750 King Richard Road
Raleigh, NC 27610

COMPUTERROOM
1729 Garden Terrace
Charlotte, NC 28203

ALTAIR COMPUTER
CENTER #3
1808 E. Independence
Charlotte, NC 28205

PROFESSIONAL COMPUTER
ASSOCIATES
126 Dogwood Lane
Kingston, NC 28501

OHIO

MICROWORKS, INC.
49 W. 5th Ave.
Columbus, OH 43201

COMPUTER DATA SYSTEMS
1372 Grandview Ave.
Columbus, OH 43212

ALTAIR COMPUTER
CENTER #4
5252 N. Dixie Dr.
Dayton, OH 45414

CYBER SHOP
1451 S. Hamilton Rd.
Columbus, OH 43227

DATA SYSTEMS
203 11th St.
Genoa, OH 43430

BYTE SHOP OF OHIO, INC.
19524 Center Ridge Rd.
Rockey River, OH 44016

ELS SMALL
COMPUTER STORE
2209 N. Taylor Rd. E.
Cleveland, OH 44112

WINTERRADIO ELECTRONIC
SUPPLY CORP.
1468 W. 25th St.
Cleveland, OH 44113

HELLER ELECTRONICS
2189 Lee Rd.
Cleveland Heights, OH 44118

CY-COMP
1154 Desert St.
Uniontown, OH 44685

DIGITAL DESIGN
7694 Camargo Rd.
Cincinnati, OH 45243

DATA DOMAIN OF DAYTON
1932 Brown St.
Dayton, OH 45409

OKLAHOMA

HIGH TECHNOLOGY
1020 W. Wilshire Blvd.
Oklahoma City, OK 73116

RADIO INC.
1000 S. Main
Tulsa, OK 74119

ALTAIR COMPUTER
CENTER
110 Annex, 5345 E. 42st
Tulsa, OK 74135

OREGON

ALTAIR COMPUTER
CENTER
8105 SW Nimbus Ave.
Beaverton, OR 97005

BYTE SHOP
COMPUTER STORE
3482 SW Cedar Hills Blvd.
Beaverton, OR 97005

BYTE SHOP OF PORTLAND
2033 SW 4th
Portland, OR 97201

PORTLAND RADIO SUPPLY
1234 SW Stark St.
Portland, OR 97205

REAL OREGON COMPUTER
CO.
205 W. 10th St.
Eugene, OR 97401

PENNSYLVANIA

CALDWELL COMPUTER CO.
546 W. Olney Ave.
Philadelphia, PA 19120

J.B. INDUSTRIES
610 W. Olney Ave.
Philadelphia, PA 19120

2005 AD INC.
2005 Naudain St.
Philadelphia, PA 19145

LECTRO-MEDIA LTD.
2nd & Pine
Philadelphia, PA 19147

LECTRO-MEDIA LTD.
22 Market St.
Philadelphia, PA 19147

PERSONAL COMPUTER
CORPORATION
Frazier Mall, Rt. 30 & 352
Frazier, PA 19355

THE ELECTRONICS PLACE
7250 McKnight Road
Pittsburgh, PA 15237

THE COMPUTER
WORKSHOP
4170 Wm. Penn Hwy. Robar Bd.
Murraysville, PA 15668

LOMBARDI ELECTRONICS
110 Ludwig Road
New Castle, PA 16105

MACE ELECTRONICS, INC.
2631 W. 8th St.
Erie, PA 16505

THE COMPUTER SHOP
116 S. Pugh St.
State College, PA 16801

MICROCOMPUTER
SYSTEMS, INC.
243 W. Chocolate Ave.
Hersey, PA 17033

ARTCO ELECTRONICS
302 Wyoming Ave.
Kingston, PA 18704

MARKETLINE SYSTEMS,
INC.
2337 Philmont Ave.
Huntingdon Valley, PA 19006

HAMTRONICS
4033 Brownsville Rd.
Trevose, PA 19047

HAM BUERGER INC.
68 N. York Rd.
Willow Grove, PA 19090

PHILADELPHIA HERITAGE
435 Spruce
Philadelphia, PA 19106

COMPUTER ROOM
1028 Spruce St.
Philadelphia, PA 19107

RHODE ISLAND

COMPUTER POWER, INC.
60 Harding St.
W. Warwick, RI 02893

SOUTH CAROLINA

DIXIE RADIO SUPPLY CO.
1900 Barnwell St.
Columbia, SC 29201

BYTE SHOP — COLUMBIA
2018 Green St.
Columbia, SC 29205

COMPUTERCO. INC.
73 State St.
Charleston, SC 29401

WORLD OF COMPUTERS
5849 Dorchester Rd.
Charleston, SC 29405

BYTE SHOP
814 Valley View Dr.
Aiken, SC 29801

TENNESSEE

BYTE'TRONICS
1600 Hayes St. #103
Nashville, TN 37203

DOC'S COMPUTER SHOP
SURYA CORP.
5755 Nolensville Rd.
Nashville, TN 37211

MICROPRODUCTS AND
SYSTEMS, INC.
2307 E. Center St.
Kingsport, TN 37664

COMPUTER DENN
1507 Oakridge Turnpike
Oakridge, TN 37830

THE COMPUTER STORE INC.
2162 Courtland Pl.
Memphis, TN 38104

TEXAS

VANGUARD SYSTEMS CORP.
6812 San Pedro
San Antonio, TX 78216

ASA COMPUTERS
5902 W. Bee Caves
Austin, TX 78746

NEIGHBORHOOD
COMPUTER STORE
#20 Terrace Shopping Ctr.
4902 34th St.
Lubbock, TX 79410

COMPUTER TERMINAL
2101 Myrtle
El Paso, TX 79901

THE COMPUTER SHOP
6812 San Pedro
San Antonio, TX 78216

KA ELECTRONIC SALES
1117 S. Jupiter Rd.
Garland, TX 75042

MICRO STORE
634 S. Central Expressway
Richardson, TX 75080

ELECTRONICS CENTER INC.
2929 N. Maskell
Dallas, TX 75204

DIGITEX
2111 Farrington
Dallas, TX 75207

ELECTRONIC SPECIALTY
CO.
2006 San Sebastian #B232
Houston, TX 77058

BYTE SHOP
3211 Fondren
Houston, TX 77063

ALTAIR COMPUTER
CENTER
12902 Harwin
Houston, TX 77072

MICROCOMPUTER ORIGIN
STORE
1853 Richmond Ave.
Houston, TX 77098

BELLAIRE ELECTRONIC
SUPPLY
5200 Bellaire Blvd.
Bellaire, TX 77401

COMPUTER CONSULTANT
101 Volney St.
So. Houston, TX 77587

PRINTING & OFFICE
SUPPLY CO.
COMPUTER CORNER
130 One Shell Plaza
Houston, TX 77002

COMPUTERTEX
2300 Richmond Ave.
Houston, TX 77006

ALTAIR COMPUTER
CENTER
Suite 206
Bintliff Dr.
Houston, TX 77036

BIT BARN
7331 Harwin, Suite 117
Houston, TX 77036

COMMUNICATION CENTERS
7231 Fondren Road
Houston, TX 77036

INTERACTIVE COMPUTERS
7646½ Dashwood
Houston, TX 77036

TANNER ELECTRONICS
11423 Harry Hines
Dallas, TX 75229

ALTAIR COMPUTER
CENTER #7
3208 Beltline Rd., Ste 206
Dallas, TX 75234

COMPUTER SHOPS, INC.
211 Keystone Park
13933 N. Central
Dallas, TX 75243

KA ELECTRONIC SALES
1220 Majesty Dr.
Dallas, TX 75247

COMPUTER PORT
926 N. Collins
Arlington, TX 76011

MULTI-INFORMATION
SYSTEMS
2710 Peachtree
Arlington, TX 76013

UTAH

MICRO COMPUTER
SYSTEMS
1403 Sandy Hills Drive
Sandy, UT 84070

MICRO-DATA SYSTEMS
796 E. Lazon Drive
Sandy, UT 84070

THE COMPUTER ROOM, INC.
3455 S.W. Temple St.
Salt Lake City, UT 84115

COMPUTER HUT
3605 Bannock St.
Salt Lake City, UT 84120

CENTRAL UTAH ELEC.
SUPPLY
735 S. State St.
Box N
Provo, UT 84601

VIRGINIA

MEDIA REACTIONS, INC.
11303 S. Shore Dr.
Reston, VA 22090

COMPUTER SYSTEMS
STORE
1984 Chain Bridge Rd.
McLean, VA 22101

MICROSYSTEMS
6605 A Backlick Rd.
Springfield, VA 22150

COMP WORKSHOP
VA INC.
5250 Port Royal Rd. #203
Springfield, VA 22151

COMPUTERS-TO-GO
4503 Broad St.
Richmond, VA 23230

COMPUTER HOBBIES
UNLIMITED
9601 Kendrick Rd.
Richmond, VA 23235

WASHINGTON

ABC COMMUNICATIONS
17550 15th Ave. NE
Seattle, WA 98155

PACIFIC COMPUTER STORE
Assocd. Frght. Frwrdrs. Yew.
Blaine, WA 98230

COMPUTER MART OF
TACOMA
4822 North 15th St.
Tacoma, WA 98405

MICROCOMPUTER
APPLICATIONS
6009-B 13th Way SE
Lacey, WA 98503

MICROCOMPUTER
APPLICATIONS
4217 Daniels St.
Vancouver, WA 98503

COMPUTER SHOP
S 107 Wall St.
Spokane, WA 99204

MICROCOMPUTER CENTER-
BYTE SHOP
1182 NE 8th
Bellevue, WA 98005

BYTE SHOP
COMPUTER STORE
14701 NE 20th Ave.
Bellevue, WA 98007

KBC COMPUTER SHOP
2735 152nd Ave.
NE Redmond, WA 98052

ALMAC/STROUM
ELECTRONICS, LASER
LINK CORP.
5811 6 Ave. S.
Seattle, WA 98108

AMATEUR RADIO
SUPPLY CO.
6213 13th Ave. S.
Seattle, WA 98108

RETAIL COMPUTER STORE
410 NE 72 St.
Seattle, WA 98115

ABC COMMUNICATIONS
17550 15th Ave. NE
Seattle, WA 98155

BYTE OF BELLEVUE
14701 N.E. 20th
Bellevue, WA 98007

MICROCOMPUTER
CENTER — BYTE SHOP
1182 NE 8th
Bellevue, WA 98005

WEST VIRGINIA

ALTAIR COMPUTER
CENTER #2
Municipal Pk. Bldg. Ste. 5
Charleston, WV 25301

COMPUTER STORE,INC.
1114 Charleston Ntl. Plaza
Charleston, WV 25301

WISCONSIN

SATTERFIELD
ELECT INC.
1900 S. Park St.
Madison, WI 53713

MICRO COMP.
785 S. Main St.
Fond du Lac, WI 54935

ITTY BITTY MACHINE CO.
2221 E. Capitol
Shorewood, WI 53211

MILWAUKEE COMPUTER
STORE
6916 W. North Ave.
Milwaukee, WI 53213

AMATEUR ELECT. SUP. INC.
4828 W. Fond Du Lac Ave.
Milwaukee, WI 53216

MILWAUKEE COMPUTER
STORE
3415 N. 49th St.
Milwaukee, WI 53216

CTC ELECTRONICS CORP.
2130 W. Clybourn St.
Milwaukee, WI 53233

AUSTIN COMPUTER
COMPANY
1835 Northgate
Beloit, WI 53511

BIT BUCKER
2689 Maple Dr.
McFarland, WI 53558

binary	octal	hex	symbol printed
0000000	0	0	NULL
.	.	.	.
.	.	.	.
.	.	.	.
0011111	37	1F	US
0100000	40	20	SPACE
0100001	41	21	!
0100010	42	22	"
0100011	43	23	#
0100100	44	24	$
0100101	45	25	%
0100110	46	26	&
0100111	47	27	'
0101000	50	28	(
0101001	51	29	)
0101010	52	2A	*
0101011	53	2B	+
0101100	54	2C	,
0101101	55	2D	-
0101110	56	2E	.
0101111	57	2F	/
0110000	60	30	0
0110001	61	31	1
0110010	62	32	2
0110011	63	33	3
0110100	64	34	4
0110101	65	35	5
0110110	66	36	6
0110111	67	37	7
0111000	70	38	8
0111001	71	39	9
0111010	72	3A	:
0111011	73	3B	;
0111100	74	3C	<
0111101	75	3D	=
0111110	76	3E	>
0111111	77	3F	?
1000000	100	40	@
1000001	101	41	A
1000010	102	42	B
1000011	103	43	C
1000100	104	44	D
1000101	105	45	E
1000110	106	46	F
1000111	107	47	G
1001000	110	48	H
1001001	111	49	I
1001010	112	4A	J
1001011	113	4B	K
1001100	114	4C	L

1001101	115	4D	M
1001110	116	4E	N
1001111	117	4F	O
1010000	120	50	P
1010001	121	51	Q
1010010	122	52	R
1010011	123	53	S
1010100	124	54	T
1010101	125	55	U
1010110	126	56	V
1010111	127	57	W
1011000	130	58	X
1011001	131	59	Y
1011010	132	5A	Z
1011011	133	5B	[
1011100	134	5C	\
1011101	135	5D	]
1011110	136	5E	^
1011111	137	5F	—
1100000	140	60	`
1100001	141	61	a
1100010	142	62	b
1100011	143	63	c
1100100	144	64	d
1100101	145	65	e
1100110	146	66	f
1100111	147	67	g
1101000	150	68	h
1101001	151	69	i
1101010	152	6A	j
1101011	153	6B	k
1101100	154	6C	l
1101101	155	6D	m
1101110	156	6E	n
1101111	157	6F	o
1110000	160	70	p
1110001	161	71	q
1110010	162	72	r
1110011	163	73	s
1110100	164	74	t
1110101	165	75	u
1110110	166	76	v
1110111	167	77	w
1111000	170	78	x
1111001	171	79	y
1111010	172	7A	z
1111011	173	7B	
1111100	174	7C	
1111101	175	7D	
1111110	176	7E	~
1111111	177	7F	DEL

IF A PRODUCT SAYS IT
SUPPLIES "64 ASCII CHARACTERS" YOU GET THESE

asc ɪɪ control characters

control	binary equivalent
(A)	0000001
(B)	0000010
(C)	0000011
(D)	0000100
(E)	0000101
(F)	0000110
(G)	0000111
(H)	0001000
(I)	0001001
(J)	0001010
(K)	0001011
(L)	0001100
(M)	0001101
(N)	0001110
(O)	0001111
(P)	0010000
(Q)	0010001
(R)	0010010
(S)	0010011
(T)	0010100
(U)	0010101
(V)	0010110
(W)	0010111
(X)	0011000
(Y)	0011001
(Z)	0011010

THE S-100 BUSS

PIN	SIGNAL
1	+8 volts power to PC boards
2	+16 volts power to PC boards
3	XRDY AND'ed with PRDY (pin 72) for 8080 RDY
4	VI0 vector interrupt request 0
5	VI1 vector interrupt request 1
6	V12 vector interrupt request 2
7	VI3 vector interrupt request 3
8	VI4 vector interrupt request 4
9	VI5 vector interrupt request 5
10	VI6 vector interrupt request 6
11	VI7 vector interrupt request 7
12	XRDY2 additional ready for CPU
13	
14	
15	still undefined
16	
17	
18	$\overline{\text{STA DSB}}$ status buffer diable
19	C/C DSB command/control buffer disabled
20	UNPROT input to memory protect circuits on memory board
21	$\overline{\text{SS comput}}$er in single-step mode
22	$\overline{\text{ADD DSB}}$ address buffer disable
23	DO DSB data out (from CPU) buffer disable
24	02 phase two clock signal
25	01 phase one clock
26	PHLDA hold acknowledge, buffered 8080 output
27	PWAIT wait acknowledge, buffered 8080 output
28	PINTE interrupt enable, buffered 8080 output
29	A5 Address line 5
30	A4 address line 4
31	A3 address line 3
32	A15 address line 15
33	A12 address line 12
34	A9 address line 9
35	D01 data out line 1
36	DO0 data out line 0
37	A10 address line 10
38	DO4 data out line 4
39	DO5 data out line 5
40	DO6 data out line 6

41	D12	data input line 2
42	D13	data input line 3
43	D17	data input line 7
44	SM1	latched 8080 M1 status
45	SOUT	latched 8080 OUT status
46	SINP	latched 8080 INP status
47	SMEMR	latched 8080 MEMR status
48	SHLTA	latched 8080 HALT status
49	CLOCK	2-MHz clock
50	GND	system ground
51	+8 volts	power to PC boards
52	-16 volts	power to board negative regulators
53	SSW DSB	sense switch disable
54	EXT CLR	clear signal for I/O devices
55	RTC	60-Hz for real-time clock
56	STS TB	strobe signal to allow status signals to be set
57	DIGI	enables CPU data input drivers
58	FRDY	used by display/control logic
59		
60		
61		
62		
63	undefined at present	
64		
65		
66		
67		
68	MWRT	write enable signal for memory
69	PS	indicates if addressed memory is protected
70	PROT	input to memory protect circuits
71	RUN	indicates computer is in run mode
72	PRDY	AND'ed with XRDY (pin 3) and goes to 8080 RDY
73	PINT	input to 8080 interrupt request
74	PHOLD	input to 8080 hold request
75	PRESET	clear signal for CPU
76	PSYNC	buffered 8080 sync signal
77	PWR	buffered 8080 write enable signal
78	PDBIN	buffered 8080 PDBIN signal
79	A0	address line 0
80	A1	address line 1
81	A2	address line 2
82	A6	address line 6
83	A7	address line 7
84	A8	address line 8

85	A13	address line 13
86	A14	address line 14
87	A11	address line 11
88	DO2	data out line 2
89	DO3	data out line 3
90	DO7	data out line 7
91	DI4	data input line 4
92	DI5	data input line 5
93	DI6	data input line 6
94	DI1	data input line 1
95	DI0	data input line 0
96	<u>SIN</u>TA	latched 8080 INTA status
97	SWO	latched 8080 WO status
98	<u>SS</u>TACK	latched 8080 STACK status
99	POC	clear signal during power up
100	GND	system ground

138

A LIST OF BOOKS TO TAKE ADVANTAGE OF:

SOFTWARE

Title	Publisher	Author
Basic BASIC	Hayden	James Coan
Advanced BASIC	Hayden	James Coan
Discovering BASIC	Hayden	James Coan
BASIC Workbook	Hayden	Kenneth Schoman
Vol. II Home Computers	Dilithium Press	Rich Didday
6800 Programming	Adam Osborne	Adam Osborne
8080 Programming	Adam Osborne	Adam Osborne
Z80 Programming	Adam Osborne	Adam Osborne
Game Playing with BASIC	Hayden	Donald Spencer

HARDWARE

Microprocessor Basics	Hayden	Michael Elphick
Vol. I Intro. to Micro-processors	Adam Osborne	Adam Osborne
Vol. II Intro. to Micro-processors	Adam Osborne	Adam Osborne
Microprocessors	Sybex	Rodney Zaks
Microprocessor Interfacing Techniques	Sybex	Rodney Zaks
Vol. 1 Home Computers	Dilithium Press	Rich Didday